SO-AAE-838

Achieving TABE® Success
in Language

Level M

 **Wright Group**

Executive Editor: Linda Kwil
Marketing Manager: Sean Klunder
Production Manager: Genevieve Kelley
Cover Designer: Vickie Tripp

ISBN 0-07-704456-8

Copyright © 2006 by The McGraw-Hill Companies, Inc. All rights reserved. No part of
this book may be reproduced, stored in a retrieval system, or transmitted in any form
or by any means, electronic, mechanical, photocopying, recording, or otherwise,
without prior permission of the publisher.

Send all inquiries to:
Wright Group/McGraw-Hill
One Prudential Plaza
130 East Randolph Street, Suite 400
Chicago, IL 60601

Printed in the United States of America.

 4 5 6 7 8 9 10 MAL 09 08 07

Table of Contents

Table of Contents continued

To the Learner

If you have had problems expressing your ideas, particularly in writing, Contemporary's *Achieving TABE® Success in Language* will help. The workbook will explain basic grammar and composition skills and let you practice those skills in focused exercises. *Achieving TABE® Success in Language* will increase your confidence in your ability to communicate, both orally and in writing.

How does using Contemporary's *Achieving TABE® Success in Language* improve your language skills, particularly writing skills? The workbook covers these areas:

- grammar and usage
- sentence formation
- paragraph development
- capitalization
- punctuation
- writing conventions for special forms, like letters and quotations

Included in the workbook are a Pretest and a Posttest. The Pretest will help you find your language strengths and weaknesses. Then you can use the workbook lessons to improve your skills. When you have finished the lessons and exercises, the Posttest will help you see if you have mastered those skills. Usually mastery means answering 80 percent of the questions correctly.

Achieving TABE® Success in Language will help you develop specific language skills, especially writing skills. The workbook is self-contained with the Answer Key at the back of the book. Clear directions will guide you through the lessons and exercises.

Each lesson in the workbook is divided into four parts.

- **The first page** clearly defines, explains, and illustrates the skill. The examples prepare you for the work in the following exercises.

- **Practice** lets you work on the skill just introduced. If a skill requires additional explanation, this page may add information.

- **Apply** gives you a different way to practice the skill.

- **Check Up** provides a quick test on the skill covered in the lesson.

How to Use This Workbook

1. Take the Pretest on pages 7–16. Check your answers with the Answer Key on page 17. Refer to the Evaluation Chart to find which skills you need to work on.

2. Take each four-page lesson one at a time. Ask your teacher for help with any problems you have.

3. Use the Answer Key, which begins on page 221, to correct your answers after each exercise.

4. At the end of each unit, read the Review and complete the Assessment. These pages provide an opportunity to combine all the individual skills you have worked on and to check your progress on them. After you finish the Assessment, your teacher may want to discuss your answers with you.

5. After you have finished all six units, take the Posttest on pages 209–219. Check your answers with the Answer Key on page 220. Then discuss your progress with your teacher.

Pretest

Decide which punctuation mark, if any, is needed in each sentence.

1. Please sign your name at the bottom of the page
      A :   **B** .   **C** ?   **D** None

2. How long will it take you to type that letter
      F ?   **G** .   **H** !   **J** None

3. Sam said "I trained to become a supervisor."
      A ?   **B** ;   **C** ,   **D** None

4. "That folder is on your desk," said the secretary.
      F "   **G** ,   **H** !   **J** None

5. I usually refuse sweet desserts however, that pie looks too good to pass up.
      A ,   **B** ;   **C** "   **D** None

6. After a long soak in the tub Mandy always felt much saner.
      F ;   **G** ,   **H** "   **J** None

7. Tonight Mom is serving brussels sprouts my least favorite vegetable.
      A ,   **B** ;   **C** "   **D** None

Choose the word or phrase that best completes each sentence.

8. Next June my brother _____ from high school.

    F graduated

    G will graduate

    H has graduated

    J had graduated

9. Of all the pieces in the museum, this one is _____.

    A older

    B more older

    C oldest

    D most oldest

10. Before we adopted our puppy, Tim _____ afraid of dogs.

    F had been

    G is

    H has been

    J be

11. Neighbors on my block _____ a barbeque.

    A is planning

    B plans

    C are planning

    D been planning

Choose the sentence in each set that is written correctly and has correct capitalization and punctuation. Be sure the sentence you choose is complete.

12. **F** Looked for the perfect gift.

    G Plays quarterback on the team.

    H The lunchroom is noisy.

    J A driver on his final run for the night.

13. **A** Milk is good for me I have some every day.

    B My car is used, it has over fifty thousand miles on it.

    C All the seats were gone.

    D The wind is strong, the sky is gray.

14. **F** "Fasten your seatbelts," said the flight attendant.

    G Did you read *The price of Love*?

    H that program were humorous.

    J One reporter was from *The Fairmount gazette*.

15. **A** Mia left her purse on the counter.

    B The Smiths painted theirs house a pale yellow.

    C Grandpa left I his gold watch.

    D As soon as them get here, we will go to the movie.

16. **F** My favorite lunch is a mexican taco salad.

    G Can I make an appointment with Dr. marshall?

    H The new director is from Phoenix, Arizona.

    J Many people travel long distances on thanksgiving day.

17. **A** Jess wouldn't take no help.

    B That burglar never leaves no fingerprints behind.

    C I can't hardly wait until tonight.

    D The local newspaper didn't print any of the articles Jack wrote.

18. **F** Just lie your keys on the table.

    G There is no need to raise your voice at me.

    H The smoke raised into the air.

    J If you are tired, lay down.

19. **A** Liz kissed her parents good-bye and waved to them from the bus.

    B The twins cooked ourselves a spicy soup.

    C Tom told itself that everything was fine.

    D The house was old and run-down, but he wasn't haunted.

20. **F** The parking meter accepts nickels dimes and quarters.

    G Mars, and Venus were visible.

    H After the play ended its run the cast had a big party.

    J I lost my job, and money is tight.

21. **A** She will visit you're father before the winter arrives.

    B Both brothers' eyes are bright blue.

    C I ca'nt find the light switch.

    D Gwens' smile faded quickly.

Read each set of underlined sentences. Then choose the sentence that best combines those sentences.

22. Troy carried the lamp all the way home.
    The lamp was heavy.

    F   Heavily, Troy carried the lamp all the way home.

    G   The lamp that Troy carried home was heavy all the way.

    H   Troy carried the heavy lamp all the way home.

    J   Troy went home, and he carried the heavy lamp all the way.

23. Erika was tired after the long hike.
    Steve was tired after the long hike.

    A   Erika was tired, and Steve was tired after the long hike.

    B   Erika and Steve were tired after the long hike.

    C   Erika was tired after the long hike, and Steve was tired after the hike, too.

    D   Tired after the long hike was Erika, and tired was Steve.

24. The hostess offered her guests lemonade.
    The hostess offered her guests cookies.

    F   The hostess offered her guests lemonade and cookies.

    G   The hostess offered her guests lemonade, and she offered them cookies.

    H   The guests had the hostess offer them cookies, and they also had the hostess offer them lemonade.

    J   The guests had lemonade offered to them, and they also had cookies offered to them by the hostess.

25. Snow fell on the city streets.
    The snow was fluffy.
    The snow was soft.

    A   The snow that fell on the city streets was soft, and it was fluffy.

    B   The city streets had snow that was soft and fluffy fall on them.

    C   Soft, fluffy snow fell on the city streets.

    D   The snow that was soft and fluffy fell on the city streets.

Read each paragraph. Then choose the sentence that best fills the blank.

26. _____. "Little Red Riding Hood" teaches children not to talk to strangers. One lesson of "The Boy Who Cried Wolf" is not to ask for help unless you really need it. "The Three Sillies" advises people not to be overly worried about the future.

    F No one knows who wrote some of the most beloved folktales and fairy tales.

    G Most people enjoy folktales and fairy tales.

    H Many folktales and fairy tales teach important lessons.

    J Folktales and fairy tales are very old stories.

27. _____. To play in the big leagues, they need fast reflexes, amazing strength and endurance, and superior muscle control. In addition, high-level sports demand an extraordinary ability to concentrate and ignore distractions.

    A All children should learn sports and games in school.

    B Top athletes must excel both physically and mentally.

    C Top athletes are paid too much money.

    D Top athletes train every day.

28. Jane steamed the wallpaper off her dining room walls. _____. Next she painted the woodwork and ceiling. Last, she and a friend put up new wallpaper. Now the room looks perfect.

    F Then she scraped off as much of the old wallpaper paste as she could.

    G Then she had a dinner party in her redecorated dining room.

    H She decided that her dining room needed a new look.

    J Then she hung pictures on the walls.

29. The scents in some perfumes come from flower petals. To get the fragrant oil, workers pass steam through the petals. The heated oil turns to gas. _____. Last, the again-liquid oil is combined with alcohol, water, and other substances to make expensive perfumes.

    A Perfume has been used for centuries for its pleasing odor.

    B First, the needed flowers are gathered.

    C Then the perfume is sold to wealthy customers.

    D Then the gas is cooled and becomes oil again.

Read each topic sentence. Then choose the answer that best develops the topic sentence.

30. The world is divided into twenty-four time zones, one for each hour of the day.

    F   There are seven continents in the world. All but one are inhabited by humans.

    G   There are sixty seconds in a minute and sixty minutes in an hour. There are seven days in a week.

    H   The zones begin at the Greenwich Meridian. When it is noon at the Greenwich Meridian, it is midnight on the other side of the world.

    J   Many people are on the new Zone diet. This diet involves eating more protein and fewer carbohydrates.

31. All cats, no matter how large or small they may be, have much in common.

    A   Some cats are golden and some are calico. Some cats, such as the Manx, which has no tail, are easy to identify.

    B   In ancient Egypt, cats were often considered to be gods. During the Middle Ages, most people in Europe were afraid of cats.

    C   Kirsten loves all kinds of cats. She has three cats of her own, and she helps out at the local humane society.

    D   All cats can climb. Every kind of cat has an excellent sense of sight, hearing, and smell. Because they are fast and quiet, cats are great hunters.

32. Not everyone agrees on whether snowmobiles should be banned from Yellowstone National Park.

    F   Yellowstone is on the borders of Wyoming, Montana, and Idaho. It was the first U.S. national park and is still the largest.

    G   Yellowstone is known for its geysers, hot springs, canyons, and mountains. Parts of it are open to visitors all year, although the winters there are long and brutal.

    H   Snowmobiles allow visitors to see parts of the park that would be otherwise impossible to reach. Those who ride snowmobiles must be cautious and follow strict rules of use.

    J   Some believe that every citizen should have the right to roam through the park on a snowmobile. Others believe that snowmobiles are too noisy and polluting to be allowed in the park.

Read each paragraph. Then choose the sentence that does not belong in the paragraph.

33.   1. Pecan trees are valuable to farmers who plant them. 2. Farmers in the United States harvest and sell about 250 million pecan nuts per year. 3. Pecan pies taste good, but they are not the ideal food for people on low-fat diets. 4. Many builders pay top dollar for pecan wood and use it to make paneling, floors, and furniture.

   A Sentence 1

   B Sentence 2

   C Sentence 3

   D Sentence 4

34.   1. A family vacation can be time for getting to know one another better. 2. The Waverly Hotel offers its guests an elegant experience. 3. The hotel lobby has lovely crystal chandeliers and comfortable chairs. 4. The staff at the Waverly treats guests with the utmost courtesy and care.

   F Sentence 1

   G Sentence 2

   H Sentence 3

   J Sentence 4

35.   1. On hot days, Lauren likes to eat cold foods. 2. Temperatures have gone over 90 degrees every day for the past week. 3. On those days, her main course is often a salad. 4. She drinks an iced tea and finishes off the meal with a dish of ice cream.

   A Sentence 1

   B Sentence 2

   C Sentence 3

   D Sentence 4

36.   1. Carlos wants his own landscaping business. 2. He enjoys caring for trees, shrubs, and flowers. 3. He feels his best when he is outdoors, working with growing things. 4. The best gardens are those that are planned carefully.

   F Sentence 1

   G Sentence 2

   H Sentence 3

   J Sentence 4

Read the following letter and paragraphs, and look at their numbered, underlined parts. Choose the answer that is written correctly for each underlined part.

(37) <u>february 10 2004</u>

Comprehensive Physicians

(38) <u>591 renfield avenue</u>

(39) <u>Wilmington, DE 19801</u>

(40) <u>Dear dr. collins,</u>

(41) On January 5, my <u>son's'</u> asthma was acting up, so I brought him in for you to examine. I have recently been billed twice for that one visit. Please have your office staff review and correct the billing as soon as possible.

(42) <u>Yours Truly:</u>

Brett Evans

Brett Evans

37. A february 10, 2004

    B February 10, 2004

    C February, 10, 2004

    D Correct as it is

38. F 591 Renfield Avenue

    G 591 Renfield avenue

    H 591, Renfield Avenue

    J Correct as it is

39. A wilmington, de 19801

    B Wilmington DE, 19801

    C Wilmington DE 19801

    D Correct as it is

40. F Dear dr. Collins;

    G Dear dr. collins:

    H Dear Dr. Collins:

    J Correct as it is

41. A sons's

    B son's

    C sons'

    D Correct as it is

42. F Yours Truly,

    G Yours truly:

    H Yours truly,

    J Correct as it is

(43) On a pleasant <u>night in April President</u> Abraham Lincoln decided
(44) to go to a play called <u>*our American cousin*</u>. The President was given a seat
      in the balcony and was enjoying the play until the third act. Suddenly
(45) a shot rang out. A Southern sympathizer, <u>John Wilkes Booth</u>, had shot the
(46) President! <u>After shooting Lincoln</u>, the President slumped in his seat. Booth
      jumped down onto the stage and made his escape, but not before hundreds of
      audience members had identified him.

43. **A** night in April, President

    B night in April: President

    C night in April; President

    D Correct as it is

45. **A** john Wilkes Booth

    B John wilkes Booth

    C John wilkes booth

    D Correct as it is

44. **F** *Our American Cousin*

    G *Our American cousin*

    H *our American Cousin*

    J Correct as it is

46. **F** Shooting Lincoln,

    G After he got done shooting,

    H After he had been shot,

    J Correct as it is

(47) Ilene <u>does'nt</u> know whether she should keep the job she has or
(48) <u>accepting</u> a new, better-paying job in another city. Moving would be
(49) <u>harder</u> on her family than keeping the old job, at least in the short run. In
      the long run, however, the job with higher pay would offer her and her
(50) children greater <u>opportunities, it</u> is a difficult decision

47. **A** doesn't

    B doesn't'

    C does'n't

    D Correct as it is

49. **A** more harder

    B hardest

    C most hardest

    D Correct as it is

48. **F** accepts

    G accepted

    H accept

    J Correct as it is

50. **F** opportunities: It

    G opportunities. It

    H opportunities it

    J Correct as it is

Read the following friendly letter and paragraphs. Notice the numbered, underlined parts. Choose the answer that is written correctly for each underlined part.

(51)   May 1; 2005

(52)   Dear Lorenzo,

(53)   How did your fishing trip go? You know, I've been thinking of you ever since you called last week. I hope you had good weather in the Gulf of Mexico for your vacation.

         We've been having a great summer here in Cleveland. Yesterday Jim and I took the kids to the Rock and Roll Hall of Fame. Do you remember how we

(54)   used to listen to Led Zeppelin records over and over? When we were kids we

(55)   thought there wasn't nothing better. It's weird to see our younger days treated as history. In fact, to our kids, it's ancient history.

         Say hello to the family. Call when you have time.

(56)   Sincerely yours

             Elizabeth

51. **A** May 1 2005

    B May 1, 2005

    C May 1. 2005

    D Correct as it is

52. **F** Dear Lorenzo:

    G Dear, Lorenzo,

    H Dear, Lorenzo

    J Correct as it is

53. **A** Ive

    B Ive'

    C i've

    D Correct as it is

54. **F** kids, we

    G kids'we

    H kids we,

    J Correct as it is

55. **A** there, wasn't nothing

    B there was nothing

    C there was anything

    D Correct as it is

56. **F** Sincerely Yours

    G Sincerely yours,

    H Sincerely yours:

    J Correct as it is

(57)   Did you know that yawning is contagious? Maybe you've noticed that
(57) when the people around <u>you yawn you</u> yawn too. Now scientists have proved that
(58) <u>chimpanzees yawns</u> contagiously too. How did they do it? Researchers in Japan
     showed chimps videotapes of other chimps yawning. Some of the chimps had
(59) young chimps with them, so the researchers tested them also. <u>However like</u>
(60) young human <u>children, them</u> didn't find yawning contagious.

57. **A** you, yawn you

    B you yawn, you

    C you yawn you,

    D Correct as it is

58. **F** chimpanzees yawn

    G chimpanzees yawned

    H chimpanzees yawning

    J Correct as it is

59. **A** However like,

    B However, like

    C However; like

    D Correct as it is

60. **F** children, their

    G children, he

    H children, they

    J Correct as it is

        Chris and Craig are fraternal twins. They don't look identical, but they do
(61) look <u>alike, the</u> same build, the same coloring, similar facial features, and so on.
(62) Most people can tell them apart, but their grandfather <u>can't hardly</u> tell one from
(63) the other. <u>Watching them grow up,</u> they always said they couldn't wait to be
(64) apart. But now that they're adults, they <u>got himself</u> an apartment together.

61. **A** alike; the

    B alike. The

    C alike: the

    D Correct as it is

62. **F** can hardly

    G cant' hardly

    H cant hardly

    J Correct as it is

63. **A** Watching them as they grew up,

    B Watching them grow up

    C Growing up,

    D Correct as it is

64. **F** got themselves

    G got ourselves

    H got oneself

    J Correct as it is

Pretest Answer Key and Evaluation Chart

This Evaluation Chart will help you find the language skills you need to study. Circle the questions you answered incorrectly and go to the practice pages covering those skills.

Key

1.	B	33.	C
2.	F	34.	F
3.	C	35.	B
4.	J	36.	J
5.	B	37.	B
6.	G	38.	F
7.	A	39.	D
8.	G	40.	H
9.	C	41.	B
10.	F	42.	H
11.	C	43.	A
12.	H	44.	F
13.	C	45.	D
14.	F	46.	H
15.	A	47.	A
16.	H	48.	H
17.	D	49.	D
18.	G	50.	G
19.	A	51.	B
20.	J	52.	J
21.	B	53.	D
22.	H	54.	F
23.	B	55.	B
24.	F	56.	G
25.	C	57.	B
26.	H	58.	F
27.	B	59.	B
28.	F	60.	H
29.	D	61.	C
30.	H	62.	F
31.	D	63.	C
32.	J	64.	F

Tested Skills	Question Numbers	Practice Pages
pronouns	15, 60	25–28, 29–32
antecedent agreement	19, 64	33–36
verbs	8, 10, 48	37–40, 41–44, 45–48
subject/verb agreement	11, 58	49–52
easily confused verbs	18	53–56
adjectives and adverbs	9, 49	57–60, 61–64, 65–68
use of negatives	17, 55, 62	69–72
sentence recognition	12, 13, 50	77–80, 81–84
sentence combining	22, 23, 24, 25	85–88, 89–92
sentence clarity	46, 57, 63	93–96, 97–100
topic sentences	26, 27	105–108, 109–112
supporting sentences	30, 31, 32	113–116, 117–120
sequence	28, 29	121–124
unrelated sentences	33, 34, 35, 36	125–128
proper nouns and proper adjectives	16, 45	137–140, 141–144
first words and titles	14, 44	145–148
end marks	1, 2	153–156
commas	6, 7, 20, 43, 54, 59	157–160, 161–164, 165–168, 169–172 173–176
semicolons and colons	5, 61	177–180
quotations	3, 4	185–188
apostrophes	21, 41, 47, 53	189–192, 193–196
business letter parts	37, 38, 39, 40, 42	201–204
friendly letter parts	51, 52, 56	197–200

Correlation Chart

Correlations Between Contemporary's Instructional Materials and TABE® Language and Language Mechanics Tests

Test 4 Language

Subskill	TABE® Form 9	TABE® Form 10	TABE® Survey 9	TABE® Survey 10	Practice and Instruction Pages			
					Achieving TABE Success in Language, Level M	*Pre-GED Language Arts, Writing*	*Complete Pre-GED*	*English Exercises (1–5)**
Usage								
pronouns	6, 9, 52	11, 48, 55		6	25–28, 29–32	30–40	46–47, 78–82	1: 19–21
antecedent agreement	14	19, 42			33–36	41–44	82	1: 22 3: 9
verb tenses	4, 7, 18, 35, 45	5, 7, 10, 54	3, 15, 20	3	37–40, 41–44, 45–48	51–66	48–49, 89–111	1: 12–18 3: 5–6
subject/verb agreement	12	39, 41		24	49–52	67–76	113–124	2: 8–18
adjectives	8, 55	6			57–60	81–94	49–50, 127–129	1: 23, 25, 27–28
adverbs	5	16		8	61–64	81–94	51–52, 130–131	1: 23, 24, 27–28
choosing between adjective/adverb	39, 46	12	21		65–68	85–86, 91	132	
using negatives	37	14, 50		21	69–72	91–92		1: 26
Sentence Formation								
sentence recognition	16, 44, 51, 54	18, 22, 44, 52	19	9, 10	77–80, 81–84	13–18	57–68	2: 3–7, 23–26 4: 9–10
sentence combining	21, 22, 23, 24	24, 25, 26, 27, 28	6, 7, 8	12, 13	85–88, 89–92	101–110	139–148	2: 19–22
Paragraph Development								
topic sentences	25, 27	30, 31, 32	9	14	105–108, 109–112	157–161	150–155	3: 15–16
supporting sentences	30	34, 35	12	16	113–116, 117–120	162–164	150–155	3: 27–28
sequence	26, 29	29	10		121–124	165–169	150–155	3: 22
unrelated sentences	31, 32	36, 37		17	125–128	165–169	150–155	3: 17–18
connectives/ transitions	28	33	11	15	129–132	101–109	139–148, 166–167	3: 19–20

Correlation Chart continued

Subskill	TABE® Form 9	TABE® Form 10	TABE® Survey 9	TABE® Survey 10	Practice and Instruction Pages			
					Achieving TABE Success in Language, Level M	Pre-GED Language Arts, Writing	Complete Pre-GED	English Exercises (1–5)*
Capitalization								
first words	38, 48	17	23		145–148		59	5: 17, 22, 25
proper nouns	13, 19, 33, 34, 53	8, 9, 15, 38, 40	13, 14	4, 5, 23, 25	137–140	23–24, 133–138	71–74	5: 18–20, 23
titles of works	36		16		145–148	134	59	5: 17, 22, 25
Punctuation								
end marks	11, 15, 49	1, 2, 13, 45	4, 24	1, 7	153–156	19–21, 139–140	59	4: 3–4
commas	2, 3, 40	3, 4, 21, 43, 49	1, 2	2, 20	157–160, 161–164, 165–168, 169–172, 173–176	141–144	142–143, 149, 166–169	4: 5–8, 11
Writing Conventions								
quotation marks	1, 20	20	5		185–188	145–146	133–134	4: 22–25
apostrophes	17, 47	23, 53	22	11	189–192, 193–196	27–28, 146, 149–150	81, 83	4: 17–19
city, state	10				173–176	143		4: 5
business letter parts	41, 42, 43, 50	46, 47, 51	17, 18, 25	18, 19, 22	201–204		105–107	5: 24

* Numbers correspond to the following titles: 1 = *Mastering Parts of Speech;* 2 = *Using Correct Sentence Structure;* 3 = *Improving Writing Style and Paragraphing;* 4 = *Building Punctuation Skills;* 5 = *Improving Spelling and Capitalization*

TABE® Forms 9 and 10 are published by CTB/McGraw-Hill. TABE is a registered trademark of The McGraw-Hill Companies.

Test 6 Language Mechanics

Subskill	TABE® Form 9	TABE® Form 10	TABE® Survey 9	TABE® Survey 10	Practice and Instruction Pages			
					Achieving TABE Success in Language, Level M	*Pre-GED Language Arts, Writing*	*Complete Pre-GED*	*English Exercises (1–5)**
Sentences, Phrases, Clauses								
first words		3		3	145–148		59	5: 17
end marks	17, 18	1, 4	17, 18	1, 4	153–156	19–21, 139–140	59–61	4: 3–4
quotation marks	1, 3, 8	2, 9, 13	1, 3, 8	2, 9, 13	185–188	145–146	133–134	4: 22–25, 5: 25
commas	2, 6, 7, 10, 19	5, 10, 18, 19, 20	2, 6, 7, 10, 19	5, 10, 18, 19, 20	157–160, 161–164, 165–168, 169–172, 173–176	141–144	142–143, 147–149, 166–169	4: 5–8, 11
Writing Conventions								
proper nouns	4, 5	7, 11	4, 5	7, 11	137–140	23–24, 133–138	71–74	5: 18–20, 23
proper adjectives	20		20		141–144			5: 18, 20
capitalize titles	11	8	11	8	145–148	134		5: 17, 22, 25
apostrophes	9, 12	12, 14	9, 12	12, 14	189–192, 193–196	27–28, 146, 149–150	81, 83	4: 17–19
city, state	16	6	16	6	173–176	143		4: 5
friendly letter parts	13, 14, 15	15, 16, 17	13, 14, 15	15, 16, 17	197–200	143–144		

* Numbers correspond to the following titles: 1 = *Mastering Parts of Speech;* 2 = *Using Correct Sentence Structure;* 3 = *Improving Writing Style and Paragraphing;* 4 = *Building Punctuation Skills;* 5 = *Improving Spelling and Capitalization*

TABE® Forms 9 and 10 are published by CTB/McGraw-Hill. TABE is a registered trademark of The McGraw-Hill Companies.

Nouns

A **noun** is a part of speech that names a person, place, or thing. Many nouns name things that can be seen or touched. Others, like *skill* and *pride*, name ideas and feelings.

Nouns are either common or proper. A **common noun** is the general name of any person, place, or thing.

> The <u>painters</u> put away their <u>brushes</u> for the <u>day</u>.

Proper nouns are the names of particular persons, places, or things. Some proper nouns are made up of more than one word. Every word in a proper noun begins with a capital letter.

> On <u>Tuesday</u>, <u>Ned</u> began painting the <u>Crane Building</u>.

Nouns can be either singular or plural. A **singular noun** names one person, place, or thing. A **plural noun** names more than one.

> This <u>wall</u> (singular) is covered with <u>layers</u> (plural) of <u>paint</u> (singular).

Underline the nouns in each sentence.

1. The company pays the manager a generous salary.

2. Ernesto survived a terrible accident on a snowy road.

3. On a trip to Texas, Nick stopped in Austin and San Antonio.

4. Jenny wore a black dress to dinner at the fancy restaurant.

5. The tall flowers waved gently in the wind.

6. The Middle Ages were a time of knights and castles.

7. The waiter treated the diners with courtesy and was rewarded with a big tip.

8. Katie had a hard time finding Depot Street on the little map.

9. Every March the Smiths travel to Palm Beach in Florida.

10. Miners came to California hoping to find gold.

Practice

Underline the singular nouns in the following paragraph. Circle the plural nouns.

      1. People all over the world can thank Charles Goodyear for a common, useful material—rubber. **2.** Although rubber was around before Goodyear, the substance was not stable. **3.** On hot days, rubber would melt and would smell bad. **4.** On cold days, rubber would become brittle and break. **5.** Goodyear believed that the substance could be made useful. **6.** After years of experiments, the inventor made a discovery. **7.** Rubber, when heated and combined with a chemical called sulfur, is stretchy and strong. **8.** To pay debts, Goodyear sold the rights to the discovery. **9.** Sadly, other people, not the inventor, became rich. **10.** Take a few moments to remember Charles Goodyear and the contribution he made.

Read each sentence. If its nouns are capitalized incorrectly, rewrite the sentence correctly on the line. If its nouns are capitalized correctly, write *Correct* on the line.

11. The citizens of new york were thrilled when the brooklyn bridge opened.

_____

12. After lauren moved into her Apartment, she sewed new Window Curtains.

_____

13. My favorite restaurant is on Bridge Street by the railroad tracks.

_____

14. The atlas mountains are located in africa.

_____

15. Eleanor roosevelt worked for the welfare of all americans.

_____

16. Steven and his family came from barbados, an island in the caribbean sea.

_____

17. Is the Fourth of July on a Monday or a Tuesday this year?

_____

Apply

Write a noun on each line to complete these sentences. Be sure it fits the description in parentheses ( ).

1. The holiday I like best is _____ (proper).

2. Fill the bowls with _____ (plural) and potato chips.

3. Beside the old house, _____ (common) and daisies grow.

4. According to the _____ (singular), that movie is opening tonight.

5. Most of the citizens voted to reelect _____ (proper) as their mayor.

6. The _____ (plural) waited silently for the starter's gun to fire.

7. When a new _____ (singular) is for sale, Gina is the first to know.

8. When the train arrived at _____ (proper), many of the passengers got off.

9. At the buffet, Frank filled his plate with _____ (common).

10. Marty got a job stacking _____ (plural) on the market's shelves.

The following story is incomplete. Several common and proper nouns are missing. On each line below, write a noun to fill in each numbered, blank line. Be sure to use a variety of common, proper, singular, and plural nouns.

Today as I was walking near the ___(11)___ , I was surprised to see a ___(12)___ . I stared for a while, not believing what I was seeing. Finally, I phoned my best friend, ___(13)___ , and told her what I had seen. She suggested that I call the ___(14)___ , so I did. Soon a crowd of ___(15)___ gathered around us. People with ___(16)___ stopped to take a look. I never saw such ___(17)___ in the city. Then reporters came, and they talked to other ___(18)___ and to me. I wonder if I will be on the news tonight.

11. _____   15. _____

12. _____   16. _____

13. _____   17. _____

14. _____   18. _____

Check Up

Choose the answer that best describes the underlined word in each sentence.

1. The <u>polls</u> will be open until 7 P.M.

   A singular noun

   B proper noun

   C plural noun

   D None of these

2. Justin and Brandy booked a room on the cruise ship <u>*Bright Voyage*</u>.

   F proper noun

   G common noun

   H plural noun

   J None of these

3. <u>Women</u> on the frontier were busy from morning until night.

   A proper noun

   B plural noun

   C singular noun

   D None of these

4. The new driver felt nervous as she <u>entered</u> the freeway.

   F plural noun

   G singular noun

   H common noun

   J None of these

5. To get to the new mall, you must cross <u>Butler Bridge</u>.

   A common noun

   B proper noun

   C plural noun

   D None of these

6. Did you read a news article about the awards <u>ceremony</u>?

   F singular noun

   G proper noun

   H plural noun

   J None of these

7. The van careened <u>down</u> the steep mountain road.

   A singular noun

   B proper noun

   C common noun

   D None of these

8. The hairdresser went to <u>Paris</u> to learn about the latest cuts.

   F common noun

   G plural noun

   H proper noun

   J None of these

9. <u>Camels</u> plodded slowly across the desert.

   A common noun

   B proper noun

   C singular noun

   D None of these

10. <u>Please</u> sign in at the desk and give your card to the receptionist.

    F plural noun

    G proper noun

    H common noun

    J None of these

Personal Pronouns

Pronouns are words used in place of nouns. There are several kinds of pronouns. One kind is the personal pronoun. **Personal pronouns** often refer to people and are used in place of their names.

> Blake had a cold, so he stayed in bed.
> (*He* refers to *Blake*.)

You can also use personal pronouns to refer to things.

> Blake turned on the TV but fell asleep in front of it.
> (*It* refers to *TV*.)

Personal pronouns are grouped in the following three ways:

Number: If the pronoun refers to one person or thing, it is singular. If it refers to more than one person or thing, it is plural.

Gender: Pronouns that refer to males are masculine (*he, him, his*). Pronouns that refer to females are feminine (*she, her, hers*). Pronouns that refer to things or animals are neuter (*it, its*).

Person: When speakers refer to themselves, they use first person pronouns. When speakers address someone else, they use second person pronouns. When speakers talk about other persons or things, they use third person pronouns.

	Singular	Plural
First Person:	I, me, my, mine	we, us, our, ours
Second Person:	you, your, yours	you, your, yours
Third Person:	he, she, him, her, it his, hers, its	they, them, their, theirs

Underline the personal pronouns in each sentence. Draw an arrow from each pronoun to the word it refers to.

1. Fiona was proud of her performance at the concert.

2. When the players ran onto the field, they waved at the fans.

3. Grandmother, do you have pictures of Dad when he was young?

4. Dana lives near her job, but she still comes in late.

5. Marvin asked, "Should I bring a notebook to the meeting?"

6. The author explained how he had done research for the book.

7. The bird has broken its wing.

Practice

The form of a personal pronoun changes depending upon how it is used.

Nominative pronouns are used as subjects of sentences and clauses.

    I   we   you   he, she, it   they

They stood in line to buy tickets.
The director thinks I will be perfect for the role.

Objective pronouns are used as objects. They can be found after verbs or after words such as *for*, *to*, or *with*.

    me   us   you   him, her, it   them

The usher led us down the aisle.
The audience clapped loudly for them.

Circle the pronoun that completes each sentence correctly.

1. The architect showed (we, us) the house plans.

2. (He, Him) will conduct the orchestra tonight.

3. Did you tell (she, her) the big news?

4. If (they, them) are late, we will have to leave without them.

5. Here are the pictures that (I, me) took on my vacation.

6. Hand in your test to (he, him).

7. Ayesha told (I, me) a good joke at lunch.

8. Kit hopes that (we, us) can come to the party.

9. The judge gave (he, him) another chance.

10. (She, Her) wanted to go on the class field trip.

11. Signs directed (they, them) to the door at the end of the hall.

12. Julia taught (she, her) the secret handshake.

13. Matt hoped that (I, me) would get the job.

14. (They, Them) were the first guests to arrive.

15. It seems to (we, us) that the mailman is coming later every day.

Apply

A possessive pronoun is a type of personal pronoun. **Possessive pronouns** show ownership.

The baby threw his cereal on the floor. (*His* refers to *baby*.)

The following is a list of possessive pronouns:

	Singular	Plural
First Person:	my, mine	our, ours
Second Person:	your, yours	your, yours
Third Person:	his, her, hers, its	their, theirs

Some possessive pronouns have two forms. One form modifies a noun (*my, our, your, her, its, their*). The other form is used by itself (*mine, ours, yours, hers, theirs*).

That is their house. That house is theirs.

The pronouns *his* and *its* do not have two forms.

This is his car. This car is his.

Remember that pronouns must match the words they refer to in gender, number, and person.

Trina writes in her diary at night.
(Both *Trina* and *her* are singular, feminine, and third person.)

Underline the possessive pronoun in each sentence. Circle the word it refers to.

1. Before the car drove off, I wrote down its license plate number.

2. Kyle used his credit card to pay for the airline tickets.

3. If the Wildcats score one more point, the game is theirs.

4. On sunny days, I like to eat my lunch on the picnic tables in back.

5. Ilene knows that someday the whole company will be hers.

On the line, write a possessive pronoun to complete each sentence.

6. Please give me _____ library card.

7. Is that painting _____?

8. _____ computer needs more memory.

9. It was _____ idea to set up chairs in the boardroom.

10. The fence between the houses is _____, not yours.

Check Up

Each sentence has one word underlined. Choose the answer that is written correctly for each underlined word.

1. The judges were impressed with yours skill.

   A yourself

   B your

   C you

   D Correct as it is

2. The speaker told they a story.

   F theirs

   G their

   H them

   J Correct as it is

3. Where are the papers that I set on this desk?

   A me

   B him

   C mine

   D Correct as it is

4. Mr. Trent believes that us can reach our goal.

   F our

   G ours

   H we

   J Correct as it is

5. Is the desk by the window hers?

   A her

   B she

   C he

   D Correct as it is

6. The city notified he about the tax increase.

   F we

   G him

   H my

   J Correct as it is

7. This may be ours last chance.

   A our

   B hers

   C us

   D Correct as it is

8. Everyone listens when her talks.

   F him

   G hers

   H she

   J Correct as it is

9. The ancient statue had lost its arm centuries ago.

   A it's

   B it

   C their

   D Correct as it is

10. The boss assigned we a new job.

   F our

   G us

   H he

   J Correct as it is

Other Kinds of Pronouns

A **relative pronoun** refers to a noun or a pronoun in the main part of the sentence. Relative pronouns include the following: *who*, *whom*, *whose*, *which*, and *that*.

Will the person whose car is blocking the driveway please move it? (*Whose* is a relative pronoun that refers to *person*.)

Who, *whom*, and *whose* refer to people. *Which* and *that* refer to things. Use *who* in front of a verb. Use *whom* after a preposition, such as *to*, *for*, and *with*.

Mary is the secretary who answers the phones. (*who* in front of the verb *answers*)
The boy for whom they are throwing the party is Jack's son. (*whom* after *for*)

A **reflexive pronoun** reflects an action back to a noun or a pronoun used earlier in the sentence. Reflexive pronouns end with *-self* or *-selves*.

	Singular	Plural
First person:	myself	ourselves
Second person:	yourself	yourselves
Third person:	himself, herself, itself	themselves

The robber let himself in by breaking a window. (*Himself* refers to *robber*.)

Underline the relative and reflexive pronouns in each sentence. Draw an arrow from each pronoun to the word it refers to.

1. The computers that we just bought are amazingly fast.

2. The driver who usually takes this route is out sick today.

3. The doctor himself called my father.

4. People today enjoy the symphony that was written in 1815.

5. The man whose son had won the prize talked to reporters.

6. The dog shook itself when it came inside.

7. The suspect whom the police had arrested was soon released.

8. Maria reminded herself to go to the cleaners.

9. The car that has a broken window is parked nearby.

10. I told myself I was going to win the lottery.

Practice

Circle the reflexive pronoun in each sentence.

1. The trapped miners reminded themselves to stay calm.

2. The workers helped themselves by joining the union.

3. The actress enjoyed herself at the cast party.

4. The baseball player congratulated himself on a game well played.

5. The secretary prides herself on being organized.

6. Ruth poured herself a big bowl of cereal.

7. The captain steadied himself before he guided the ship into the harbor.

8. You should give yourself a pat on the back.

9. I convinced myself to sing in the talent show.

10. You helped yourself to several of the appetizers on the tray.

Circle the relative or reflexive pronoun in each sentence. On the line, write **REL** if the pronoun is relative or **REF** if it is reflexive.

11. _____ Can you disconnect the phone that has been ringing all day?

12. _____ The suitcase that Mary uses on business trips was lost by the airline.

13. _____ The president helped himself in the polls by supporting a tax cut.

14. _____ Tina was proud of herself when she was named Employee of the Month.

15. _____ Did Tim pick up the package that came for him yesterday?

16. _____ The employees helped themselves to seconds at the company picnic.

17. _____ Ginelle loved the drawing that her daughter made for her at school.

18. _____ I am fond of my neighbor who always gives me herbs from her garden.

19. _____ Mitch is the paralegal who shares an office with Natalie.

20. _____ Shirley is the person to whom the letter is addressed.

Apply

Underline the pronoun that completes each sentence correctly.

1. Max saved (himself, herself) a piece of the chocolate cream pie.

2. The amusement park prides (itself, yourself) on having the largest roller coaster.

3. My baby waves hello to (herself, itself) in the mirror.

4. The principal, (who, whom) was a former teacher, treats her staff well.

5. (Who, Whom) will volunteer to clean up the park with us?

6. They gather (ourselves, themselves) together to admire the roses they had planted.

7. She gave (myself, herself) the job of cooking the Thanksgiving turkey.

8. The operator (who, that) took my call had a pleasant voice.

9. We should give (ourselves, yourselves) plenty of time to reach the meeting.

10. With (who, whom) are you going to the concert?

Follow the instructions for each item.

11. Write a sentence using the relative pronoun *who*.

    _____

12. Write a sentence using the relative pronoun *whom*.

    _____

13. Write a sentence using the relative pronoun *that*.

    _____

14. Write a sentence using the reflexive pronoun *myself*.

    _____

15. Write a sentence using the reflexive pronoun *themselves*.

    _____

16. Write a sentence using the reflexive pronoun *yourself*.

    _____

Check Up

In each sentence, a pronoun is underlined. Choose the answer that is written correctly for each underlined pronoun.

1. The actor turned <u>itself</u> into a movie star.

   A herselves

   B himself

   C themselves

   D ourselves

2. <u>Whom</u> has your e-mail address?

   F Who

   G Which

   H That

   J Whose

3. My cousin was in a play <u>which</u> ran on Broadway.

   A who

   B that

   C whose

   D whom

4. The hostess outdid <u>themselves</u> at the luncheon.

   F ourselves

   G himself

   H yourself

   J herself

Choose the phrase that identifies the underlined pronoun in each sentence.

5. The conductor proved to <u>himself</u> that he could lead the orchestra.

   A singular and feminine

   B third person and masculine

   C plural and masculine

   D third person and neuter

6. We left <u>ourselves</u> enough time to make a special dinner.

   F first person and plural

   G first person and singular

   H second person and plural

   J third person and plural

7. You should not blame <u>yourself</u> for the accident.

   A second person and plural

   B third person and plural

   C second person and singular

   D first person and singular

8. The team members gave <u>themselves</u> a rousing cheer.

   F third person and singular

   G second person and singular

   H third person and plural

   J first person and plural

Making Pronouns Agree with Their Antecedents

The word a pronoun replaces is called its **antecedent**.

> Jason plays his guitar every evening.

> (The antecedent of the pronoun *his* is *Jason*.)

Pronouns must agree with their antecedents in number. A pronoun that refers to a singular antecedent must be singular. A pronoun that refers to a plural antecedent must be plural.

> The actress blew kisses to her fans. (singular)

> Police controlled the fans by keeping them behind ropes. (plural)

Pronouns must also agree with their antecedents in gender. Pronouns and antecedents may be masculine (*he, him, his*), feminine (*she, her, hers*), or neuter (*it, its*).

> The soldier wrote a letter to his mother. (masculine)

> That singer writes all her own songs. (feminine)

> I need my wallet because it contains my license. (neuter)

Circle the antecedent of the underlined pronoun in each sentence. Identify the number of the pronoun and its antecedent. On the line, write *S* for singular or *P* for plural.

1. _____ The diners had to wait over fifteen minutes for their check.

2. _____ Kris enjoys visiting the pandas at the zoo because they are so cute.

3. _____ The landscaper hired Brad as her assistant.

4. _____ Ray likes oatmeal and makes it for himself every morning.

Circle the antecedent of the underlined pronoun in each sentence. Identify the gender of the pronoun and its antecedent. On the line, write *M* for masculine, *F* for feminine, or *N* for neuter.

5. _____ Sara wanted a leather jacket but couldn't afford it.

6. _____ Dan brings his lunch to work every day.

7. _____ Karen looked forward to Friday night, when she would see her friends.

8. _____ John bought the book because it had gotten good reviews.

Practice

Pronouns must also agree with their antecedents in person. You use first person when you talk about yourself. You use second person when you talk to someone else. You use third person when you talk about other persons or things.

    I picture myself as a world traveler. (first person)

    You yourself can be the judge. (second person)

    Maria and her sisters went on a cruise. (third person)

It is important to make relative pronouns agree with their antecedents, too. Use *who* and *whom* when the antecedents are people. Use *which* and *that* when the antecedents are not people.

    The artist who painted this picture has moved to New York. (The *artist* is a person.)

    The dress was made of silk that had come from China. (*Silk* is a thing.)

Circle the antecedent of the underlined pronoun in each sentence. Identify the person of the pronoun and its antecedent. On the line, write *1* for first person, *2* for second person, or *3* for third person.

1. _____ When Hector visits the doctor's office, he takes along a good book.

2. _____ I am surprised that Elaine remembered my birthday.

3. _____ The protesters held up their signs and shouted at the speaker.

4. _____ You may set your wet clothes by the fire to dry.

5. _____ Because Margot loves peaches, she buys them by the peck.

Underline the pronoun that correctly completes each sentence. Circle its antecedent.

6. Sean slowed down when (it, he) saw the flashing lights ahead.

7. The homeowner (which, whose) garden was pictured in the paper felt proud.

8. The astronauts put on (his, their) space suits and waited for the signal to board.

9. Kelly and Celeste locked (ourselves, themselves) out of their car.

10. The bear ran back into (their, its) cave where it felt safe.

11. Laura has asked (his, her) brother to usher at the wedding.

12. The home, (who, which) was built in 1924, was filled with antiques.

13. I (himself, myself) can't remember the address.

14. Steve bought bagels and shared (it, them) with his coworkers.

Apply

Read each sentence. If it has a pronoun that does not agree with its antecedent, rewrite the sentence correctly on the line. If there is antecedent agreement, write *Correct*.

1. After Mike got his paycheck, he deposited them in the bank.

   _____

2. The flight was scheduled for take-off an hour ago, but it has been delayed.

   _____

3. The cows slowly lifted her heads when the farmer approached.

   _____

4. The king and her court enjoyed the juggler's act.

   _____

5. The prize should go to the dancer that wore the red costume.

   _____

6. We knocked on the door, but the guard would not let us in.

   _____

7. Grandmother is proud of his grandchildren.

   _____

8. Mia drove slowly because you could barely see through the fog.

   _____

9. Please give me the files so I can study it.

   _____

10. Fans begged the actress for its autograph.

    _____

Check Up

Choose the pronoun that best completes each sentence.

1. Justin bought a dozen roses for _____ girlfriend.

   A their

   B his

   C her

   D its

2. A writer _____ interviewed the mayor wrote this article.

   F who

   G whom

   H which

   J that

3. Before you receive _____ lunch, you must pay the cashier.

   A our

   B. his

   C your

   D their

4. Alicia finished last but was still pleased with _____.

   F myself

   G herself

   H themselves

   J ourselves

5. Russ learned a new song, and he played _____ for the family.

   A it

   B them

   C him

   D they

6. Lifeguards must stay at _____ posts until the pool closes.

   F his

   G her

   H its

   J their

Read each set of sentences. Then choose the sentence that is written correctly.

7. A The man who got the job will start tomorrow.

   B I will catch the train who gets in at noon.

   C The person to which you should speak will be back shortly.

   D He is the officer that wrote the ticket.

8. F Ned and Jim wanted to come, but he had to work.

   G A student must make their own course choices in the fall.

   H David is going back to school to get more training in his field.

   J Lisa wrote several letters and sent it to the governor.

Verbs

Verbs are words that name actions or states of being. You will find at least one verb in every sentence. **Action verbs** show action being done by the subject.

> Opal studies during lunch hour.

Some verbs that show state of being are **linking verbs.** Some common linking verbs are *am, is, are, was,* and *were.* A linking verb links a noun with another noun, pronoun, or adjective.

> Mr. Venn is Opal's teacher. (*Is* links *Mr. Venn* and *teacher.*)
>
> Mr. Venn is older than Opal. (*Is* links *Mr. Venn* and *older.*)
>
> Mr. Venn is in the office today. (no link)

A few verbs are used as **helping verbs** with other verbs. Use *has, have, can, would, should, must, might, may, did, does, will,* and *shall* before the base form of another verb. This creates a **verb phrase.**

> Staff members *can* earn raises through their studies.
>
> Opal *has found* new self-confidence through her classes.

Underline every verb and verb phrase in each sentence.

1. Many neighborhoods lost electricity during the storm.

2. In past years, door-to-door salesmen were a common sight.

3. The pianist struck the keys forcefully.

4. The bus leaves in ten minutes, so we must buy tickets quickly!

5. Carol reads every book that is a choice of her book club.

6. Who was the first female airplane pilot?

7. I often attend plays here because tickets are cheap, and the acting is surprisingly good.

8. The newscaster stumbled over several unfamiliar names.

9. Our car was repaired by noon.

10. Snow fell quietly through the night and covered all the streets.

Practice

Every verb has forms called **principal parts.** The chart below names the three principal parts and gives some examples.

Present Tense	Past Tense	Past Participle
count	counted	(has) counted
smile	smiled	(has) smiled
ride	rode	(has) ridden
fly	flew	(has) flown

A verb is a **regular verb** if its past tense and past participle are both formed by adding -*ed* or -*d* to the present tense form. In the chart, *count* and *smile* are examples of **regular verbs.** A verb is an **irregular verb** if its principal parts do not follow that pattern. Both *ride* and *fly* are irregular verbs.

The following chart lists three important irregular verbs. These three verbs are used as both main verbs and helping verbs.

Present Tense	Past Tense	Past Participle
be	was, were	(has) been
do	did	(has) done
have	had	(has) had

Twelve verbs are listed below. In the paragraph, underline a form of each of the listed verbs. On the line write *R* if it is a regular verb or *IR* if it is an irregular verb.

     I have never forgotten my first experience with cooking. I meant to make a soufflé for Sunday brunch. The cookbook directions said to separate the yolks from six eggs. I broke the eggs over a bowl and then tried to scoop out the yolks. The menu quickly changed to scrambled eggs. I accidentally left pieces of shell in the eggs. When I cut the melon, I cut myself, too. I burned the toast. The meal looked like the rubble after a fire. When I served my masterpiece, I thought my parents would never stop laughing.

1. burn   _____

2. think   _____

3. try   _____

4. cut   _____

5. forget   _____

6. leave   _____

7. break   _____

8. mean   _____

9. change   _____

10. say   _____

11. look   _____

12. serve   _____

Apply

Underline the verb in each sentence. On the line, write *action* if it is an action verb or *linking* if it is a linking verb.

1. That company sponsored the program. _____

2. Many tourists travel to the Washington Monument each year. _____

3. Grandmother Harris is my mother's mother. _____

4. The government sold liberty bonds during World War I. _____

5. The long drought has ruined this year's corn crop. _____

6. Cowboys guarded herds of cattle against mountain lions and rustlers.

   _____

7. The Ellison brothers are the best house painters available. _____

Choose the helping verb that best completes each sentence.

8. Americity _____ be Melanie's new employer.

   A is

   B are

   C will

9. Janet _____ traveling with Tom.

   F can

   G has

   H is

10. Hailey's coat _____ torn on a nail.

    A were

    B was

    C had

11. Tracy _____ move to a new apartment in the spring.

    F can

    G is

    H has

12. Joan and Camille _____ attend their high school reunion.

    A is

    B were

    C will

13. Lisa _____ elected the captain of our basketball team.

    F was

    G will

    H can

Check Up

Choose the verb or verb phrase that best completes each sentence.

1. For dinner tonight we _____ pizza.

   A has eaten

   B will eat

   C will ate

   D eats

2. The accident _____ traffic on the highway.

   F stopped

   G stop

   H have stopped

   J will have stopped

3. In the book *Peter Pan*, children _____.

   A can fly

   B flies

   C has flown

   D can flown

4. The early explorers _____ treasure-seekers.

   F is

   G was

   H were

   J are

Read each set of sentences. Choose the sentence that is written correctly and makes the most sense.

5. **A** I lose my keys in my purse.

   B I lost my keys in my purse.

   C I had lost in my purse by my keys.

   D My keys lost in my purse.

6. **F** My boss must flew to California next week.

   G My boss flied to California last week.

   H California had flown by my boss last week.

   J My boss must fly to California next week.

7. **A** Gilbert Stuart drawn this portrait.

   B Gilbert Stuart draw this portrait.

   C Gilbert Stuart had drawn by this portrait.

   D Gilbert Stuart drew this portrait.

8. **F** The view from the porch has beautiful.

   G The view from the porch is beautiful.

   H The view from the porch are beautiful.

   J The view from the porch beautiful.

Simple Tenses of Verbs

The form of a verb changes to show the time of its action. A verb's different forms are its **tenses**. Three tenses—present, past, and future—are called the **simple tenses**.

Present: I hear a siren. The siren sounds close.

Past: It sounded far away a few minutes ago.

Future: It will sound louder very soon.

Use the **present tense** for an action that happens now or on a regular basis, as in "Ambulances speed to the emergency room." The present tense forms of most verbs follow the pattern shown below for *work*. The forms of *have, be,* and *do* are different.

work: I work, you work, he works, we work, they work

have: I have, you have, she has, we have, they have

be: I am, you are, it is, we are, they are

do: I do, you do, she does, we do, they do

Use the **past tense** for an action that happened in the past. The past tense is the second principal part of a verb. For the past tense of a regular verb, add *-ed* or *-d* to the present tense form. To find the past tense of an irregular verb, see a dictionary. The verb *be* has two past tense forms: *was* (singular) and *were* (plural).

Use the **future tense** for an action that has not yet happened but will occur in the future. The future tense is formed by using a helping verb such as *will* or *shall* with the present tense form.

Underline every verb or verb phrase in each sentence. Identify the tense of each verb by writing _Present_, _Past_, or _Future_ on the line.

1. Some fans will pay any price for a Super Bowl ticket. _____

2. Who disagrees with the proposal? _____

3. Amir picked the ripest tomatoes on his plants. _____

4. Usually, Marcia's husband fixes whatever breaks. _____

5. I will stop at the supermarket on my way home. _____

6. Before we had refrigerators, someone delivered ice to homes. _____

7. Your appointment book looks full. _____

8. Because his best friend moved away, Abner is lonely. _____

Practice

Read each pair of sentences. Then choose the sentence that uses the correct form of the verb and makes the most sense.

1. **A** Charles served in the Union Army for a year.

   B The explosion of a nearby cannon will kill Charles on July 18, 1864.

2. **A** The parade will begin at exactly 10 A.M.

   B World War II will end in 1945.

3. **A** We flew cars in the year 2050.

   B Maybe cars will fly in the year 2050.

4. **A** The teens drive through downtown yesterday.

   B Yesterday I saw my cousin Fernando.

5. **A** On June 16, all of Lisa's friends will attend her wedding.

   B Probably her mom will cried through the wedding ceremony.

6. **A** Jeff will wash dishes during the commercials last week.

   B The station broadcasts one ad after another.

7. **A** Several large bushes leaned over the sidewalk.

   B Last week we file a complaint about the situation.

8. **A** The cab driver will honked once in front of the building.

   B The cabbie waits for her customers.

9. **A** The student hopes to study abroad in England.

   B Jeannette has a bad attendance record last year.

10. **A** Tomorrow was Johnny's sixteenth birthday.

    B The construction workers will begin work on Thursday.

Apply

Choose the correct form of the verb to complete each sentence. Write it on the line.

1. sing　　　　sang　　　will sing

   A A cell phone rang the whole time that the choir _____.

   B Mary _____ in the concert next May.

2. see　　　　saw　　　will see

   A While the Kents were traveling in Hawaii, they _____ a volcano.

   B I _____ John walking his dog every morning.

3. fights　　　fought　　will fight

   A Tom _____ to stay awake during his 8 A.M. class tomorrow.

   B The Union soldiers and Southern confederates _____ during the Civil War.

4. spill　　　spilled　　will spill

   A Stop using that pitcher! You _____ cream all over!

   B Natalia _____ soda all over her new dress.

5. reads　　　read　　　will read

   A Often, Lucia _____ the last pages of a mystery novel before reading the middle of the book.

   B Carolyn _____ that book when she was in college.

Underline the correct tense of the verb to complete each sentence.

6. Martha (explain, will explain) the new computer program next Tuesday.

7. Julio (traveled, will travel) to New Orleans last month on business.

8. Amy told her father that she still (wants, wanted) to speak at her upcoming graduation in June.

9. Aman (returned, will return) to India next June to visit his parents.

10. The meteorologists are predicting that we (experienced, will experience) a mild winter this year.

Check Up

Choose the verb or verb phrase that best completes each sentence.

1. The planning committee _____ next week.

   A will meet

   B has met

   C met

   D meet

2. The family _____ to Niagara Falls about a month ago.

   F drove

   G will drive

   H drive

   J drives

3. Sometime tomorrow evening, my friend from Texas _____.

   A has arrived

   B will arrive

   C arrive

   D arrived

4. I _____ well in the race yesterday.

   F will do

   G did

   H do

   J has done

Read each set of sentences. Pay special attention to verbs and their tenses. Choose the sentence that is written correctly.

5. A The Petersons enjoys their last day of vacation.

   B As Matt Peterson stroll along the beach, his father will set up the grill.

   C Mrs. Peterson returned from a last swim.

   D The family has gone home tomorrow.

6. F Was Teddy Roosevelt our most colorful president?

   G Before he took office, T. R. becomes a hero during a war.

   H When his family lived in the White House, his boys will lead a horse up its steps.

   J In 1906, Teddy receives the Nobel Peace Prize.

7. A One night Dora will sit on the back porch and watched birds.

   B The birds walk and hop across the lawn as they looked for food.

   C While Dora sat, the birds moved closer and closer toward her.

   D When the door slammed, the birds fly away.

8. F For thousands of years, people use ice to keep food cold.

   G In the 1800s, inventors will develop the first refrigerators.

   H After a special liquid takes heat from inside a refrigerator, it changed to a gas.

   J When the gas flows to pipes outside the refrigerator, it loses the heat.

Perfect Tenses of Verbs

Action that is completed by a certain time is expressed in a **perfect tense.** Every perfect tense verb has at least two words: a simple tense form of *have* and the past participle of the main verb. (Remember that the simple tense forms of *have* are as follows: present—*has, have*; past—*had*; future—*will have*.)

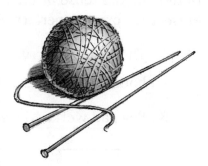

Use the **present perfect tense** to express action that began in the past. The action may now be complete or continuing.

> Emma <u>has knitted</u> since she was a child. (continuing)
>
> I <u>have received</u> a handmade scarf from her. (complete)

Use the **past perfect tense** to express action that was completed before another action in the past.

> She <u>had knitted</u> many articles <u>before she began high school</u>.

Use the **future perfect tense** to express action that will be completed before a time or action in the future.

> She <u>will have knitted</u> another sweater <u>by the end of this year</u>.

At least one verb in each item below is in a perfect tense. Underline every verb or verb phrase in the item. Then write each perfect tense verb on the line.

1. Last week the bus company changed the times that my bus runs. Riders had complained about the old schedule. _____

2. Vincent has collected fifty items for the museum's fundraising auction this week. By April, he will have donated fifty volunteer hours. _____

3. Crystal has offered us a ride to the airport, but our luggage probably will not fit in her tiny trunk. _____

4. Paco had hired Passable Painters before he received a price quote.

   _____

5. Jenise and Arthur have exchanged e-mail daily for over three years, ever since they met. _____

6. Marc will sell his car next spring. By then, he will have put over 86,000 miles on it.

   _____

Practice

Determine the tense of the underlined verb in each sentence. On the line, write *Present* for present perfect, *Past* for past perfect, and *Future* for future perfect.

1. **A** The customer service representative <u>has answered</u> at least fifteen calls this hour. _____

   B Bev <u>had worked</u> in sales before she became a customer service rep. _____

   C Before the end of her shift, Bev <u>will have answered</u> over 100 calls today. _____

2. **F** Until a stray cat followed him home, Jack <u>had considered</u> cats unfriendly. _____

   G To this day, Jack's opinion of cats <u>has not changed</u>. _____

   H By year's end, Jack <u>will have advised</u> almost all of his friends to get cats. _____

3. **A** By the end of the month, the book club at the library <u>will have discussed</u> the book *1984*. _____

   B No one <u>had dreaded</u> the arrival of the year 1984 before the book was published. _____

   C The book's author <u>had predicted</u> events before people were ready to accept what might happen in the future. _____

Underline the correct form of the verb to complete each sentence.

4. The children (has washed, had washed) the dishes before they went outside to play.

5. Christine (has sang, has sung) in a choir since she was five years old.

6. I (has received, have received) a birthday present from Anna.

7. Joe (had bought, will have bought) his wife a new pair of earrings by the time the holidays arrive.

8. By tomorrow night Heather (had finished, will have finished) her report.

Apply

Read each pair of sentences. Choose the sentence that uses the correct verb tense.

1. **A** The man had lost five bets before he gave up gambling for good.

   B The man had been losing five bets before he gave up gambling for good.

2. **A** Since the tornado had knocked the tower down, homes in this area will not received television signals.

   B Since the tornado knocked the tower down, homes in this area have not received television signals.

3. **A** At the end of the coming season, our shortstop will have played for 17 years.

   B At the end of the coming season, our shortstop had played for 17 years.

4. **A** My office plants had looked sick before I moved them off the windowsill.

   B My office plants has looked sick before I moved them off the windowsill.

Complete each sentence with a perfect tense form of the verb in parentheses.

5. (plan) The detective learned that the suspect _____ a trip before she suddenly disappeared.

6. (grab) Before his parents rushed him out, that little boy _____ the ears of half the animals in the petting zoo.

7. (complete) By bedtime tonight, Angela _____ most of the crossword puzzles in her new book.

8. (stand) That bookcase _____ in that corner ever since we moved into the house.

9. (clear) By the time this blizzard ends tomorrow, snowplows _____ roads nonstop for five days.

10. (use) We _____ fans for five hours by the time someone comes to fix the air-conditioning.

Check Up

Choose the verb or verb phrase that best completes each sentence.

1. By the time he leaves the buffet table, Johnnie _____ a helping of every food available.

    A will have taken

    B will have take

    C will have took

    D took

2. I found that Steve _____ me before I had returned from vacation.

    F has called

    G will have called

    H had called

    J have called

3. Just before the storm hit, the temperature _____ sharply.

    A have dropped

    B will have dropped

    C has dropped

    D had dropped

4. Edna _____ songs for her family since she was five years old.

    F have sung

    G had sung

    H will have sung

    J has sung

Read each set of sentences, paying special attention to verbs and their tenses. Choose the sentence that is written correctly.

5. A Before we moved here, we has lived in an apartment.

    B When we took the apartment, we have just moved here from Ohio.

    C At the end of August, we will have lived here six years.

    D We will have appreciated the nearby bus line.

6. F Ginny will have complained about dorm food all year.

    G Before she came to the dorm, she have complained about the food at home.

    H Everyone have heard her gripes.

    J Nevertheless, she has not lost weight this year.

7. A Today, Elmo learned that library fines have changed a week ago.

    B Before the change, the library had charged two cents per day for overdue books.

    C Since last Thursday, the fine will have been five cents per day.

    D By next Monday, his fines will have climb above five dollars.

8. F For some time, Willa have kept the office bulletin board free of clutter.

    G Managers have leaved their notices of meetings up for months.

    H Recently her job have become easier.

    J The reason is that managers have switched to e-mail.

Agreement of Subjects and Verbs

Every verb in the present tense changes form to show number. Usually, the plural form of a verb is its present tense form. This form is used with a plural subject.

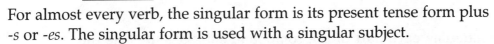

Bus drivers <u>face</u> many challenges.

Also use the plural form of a verb with *I* and *you*.

I <u>remember</u> some drivers better than others.

You <u>appreciate</u> helpful drivers.

For almost every verb, the singular form is its present tense form plus -*s* or -*es*. The singular form is used with a singular subject.

A bus driver <u>handles</u> problems with traffic and passengers daily.

Remember the following exceptions to these rules:

- The plural form of *be* is *are* (*we are, you are, they are; girls are*).

- *Be* has two singular forms, *am* and *is*. Use *am* with *I* (*I am*). Use *is* with all other singular subjects (*he is, she is, it is; Riley is*).

- The singular form of the verb *have* is *has* (*he, she,* or *it has; Hailey has*). The plural form is *have* (*they have; boys have*).

Decide whether the correct verb form is used in each sentence. If it is not, write the correct form on the line. If the verb is correct, write *Correct*.

1. Some grasses grow well in shade. _____

2. Those shoes goes on sale next week. _____

3. My cat am a Siamese. _____

4. Rolf's father works as a teller. _____

5. The porch windows need a thorough washing. _____

6. On Tuesday evenings I is at my yoga class. _____

7. Self-confident people tries almost anything. _____

8. The city prune the trees in the park on request. _____

9. Those three cats sits in the windows. _____

10. The basketball is slightly flat. _____

Practice

A **compound subject** has two or more parts. When the parts of the subject are joined by *and*, a plural verb is needed.

> Gail and her brother suffer from allergies.

If the parts of a compound subject are joined by *or* or *nor*, make the verb agree with the part closest to the verb.

> Pet hair or certain foods cause bad reactions. (The plural subject *foods* is closer to the verb, so the verb is plural.)

> Neither Gail's parents nor her sister has any allergic reaction to these things. (The singular subject *sister* is closer to the verb, so the verb is singular.)

In each sentence, underline each part of the compound subject and circle the word (*and*, *or*, or *nor*) joining the parts. Then underline the correct verb form in parentheses. On the line, write *S* if the verb is singular or *P* if it is plural.

1. Both the book and the movie script (am, is, are) by the same writer. _____

2. Either that chain or the independent stores (carries, carry) my brand. _____

3. Neither the hanging lamps nor the ceiling fixture (gives, give) enough light.
   _____

4. A dozen pennies and one dime (makes, make) my change purse heavy. _____

5. No matter what problems happen on this tour, the Cabot sisters or Mr. Van Ness (has, have) the solution. _____

Complete each sentence by writing the correct present tense form of the verb in parentheses.

6. (be) Either the signposts or your map _____ wrong.

7. (be) Deborah's red shoes and her white sweater _____ new.

8. (show) Neither the tomatoes nor the squash _____ any sign of frost.

9. (sit) Usually, Grandpa or the two cats _____ in that chair.

10. (watch) Parents and the lifeguard _____ toddlers in the wading pool.

11. (call) Often, the players or the referee _____ for time out.

12. (slide) Neither our sled nor our skis _____ on this rough ice.

Apply

Frequently a phrase comes between the subject of a sentence and its verb. The verb should agree with the subject, not the last word in the phrase.

The milk in these bottles has turned sour. (The subject is *milk*, a singular noun. The verb must be singular.)

Trucks carrying the milk were delayed. (The subject is *trucks*, a plural noun. The verb must be plural.)

To decide whether a verb should be singular or plural, first find the subject. Think of the sentence without the words between the subject and the verb. Then choose the right verb form.

Problem: Donations to this charity (is, are) tax-deductible.

Process: The subject is *Donations*. Think of the sentence as Donations (is, are) tax-deductible.

Solution: Donations to this charity are tax-deductible.

In each sentence, identify the subject. On the line, write only the subject and the correct verb form from the parentheses.

1. The problem causing many paper jams (is, are) too much moisture in the paper.

   _____

2. Prices for this cruise (has, have) been lowered significantly.

   _____

3. Children waiting for the school bus (was, were) soaked in the sudden downpour.

   _____

4. Photographs of the valley rarely (captures, capture) its grandeur.

   _____

5. During the gold rush, only one out of every twenty miners (was, were) successful.

   _____

6. The questions on this quiz (tricks, trick) almost everyone.

   _____

7. Dorothy, unlike her parents, (has, have) always been adventurous.

   _____

Check Up

Choose the verb or verb phrase that best completes each sentence.

1. Many evenings, leftovers _____ a fast dinner.

   A provides

   B has provided

   C provide

   D is providing

2. Persistence despite difficulties often _____ success.

   F bring

   G brings

   H have brought

   J are bringing

3. Both a tornado and a hurricane _____ wind damage.

   A is causing

   B has caused

   C causes

   D cause

4. Cut flowers or a plant _____ a nice gift for the hostess.

   F makes

   G have made

   H make

   J are making

Read each set of sentences. Choose the sentence in which the subject and verb agree.

5. A Letters asking for money makes up most of my mail.

   B Either several tacks or a nail hold this poster in place.

   C The orchestra members and the conductor works well together.

   D Most U.S. presidents have been reelected to a second term.

6. F Blood-sucking mosquitoes is the worst thing about summer.

   G Either the two portraits or the still life is perfect for that wall.

   H Neither the still life nor the two portraits is for sale.

   J Pieces of candy fills the little boy's Halloween bag.

7. A Has anyone here read any Sherlock Holmes stories?

   B Photos of old wallpaper inside the old house was helpful in restoring the building.

   C Several French tourists and their guide has arrived at the museum.

   D Probably, a thick wad of leaves block the drain.

8. F Games that require patience does not appeal to Henry.

   G Peanut butter or hot dogs satisfies my children anytime.

   H Neither the roller coasters nor the Ferris wheel operates in rain.

   J Either Miriam or her friends attends every game.

Easily Confused Verbs

Often speakers and writers become confused when they use certain pairs of verbs that sound alike or have similar meanings. Especially in formal or business situations, it is important to use these verbs correctly.

***Rise* and *Raise*:** *Rise* means "to go up." *Raise* means "to lift something." *Raise* is always followed by an object.

> Smoke <u>rises</u> from the fire.
> Last night, smoke <u>rose</u> from the fire.
>
> <u>Raise</u> the window a little. (*Window* is the object.)
> An hour ago, she <u>raised</u> the window.

***Lie* and *Lay*:** *Lie* means "to rest or recline." *Lay* means "to set or put something down." *Lay* is always followed by an object.

> <u>Lie</u> down before dinner.
> Yesterday, he <u>lay</u> down before dinner.
> He <u>has lain</u> down before dinner every night this week.
>
> <u>Lay</u> the quilt on the bed. (*Quilt* is the object.)
> An hour ago, she <u>laid</u> the quilt on the bed.
> She <u>had laid</u> it on the sofa earlier.

***Teach* and *Learn*:** *Teach* means "to instruct." *Learn* means "to gain knowledge or skill." You *teach* someone how to do something. The person *learns* the skill.

> Mrs. Randall <u>will teach</u> you how to knit.
> Last year, she <u>taught</u> me how to knit.
> You <u>will learn</u> how to knit.

Write each word beside its meaning.

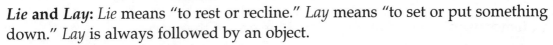

lay   lie   learn   raise   rise   teach

1. _____ to set something down

2. _____ to go up

3. _____ to instruct

4. _____ to lift something

5. _____ to recline

6. _____ to gain skill or knowledge

Practice

Read each pair of sentences. Then choose the sentence in which the verb is used correctly.

1. **A** The owner raised the price of his house.

   B The owner rose the price of his house.

2. **A** Sara laid her baby on the changing table.

   B Sara lay her baby on the changing table.

3. **A** I learned myself how to dance from a book.

   B I taught myself how to dance from a book.

4. **A** Audience members rose to their feet at the end of the concert.

   B Audience members raised to their feet at the end of the concert.

5. **A** Michelle is teaching to speak German.

   B Michelle is learning to speak German.

6. **A** Sean's sunburn told us that he had laid in the sun too long.

   B Sean's sunburn told us that he had lain in the sun too long.

For each sentence, underline the correct verb in parentheses ( ).

7. (Lay, Lie) very still until the X-ray has been taken.

8. Will you (teach, learn) us the words to the song?

9. The temperature usually (rises, raises) after noon.

10. Yesterday, we (laid, lay) on the beach for hours.

11. Mr. Gibson has (raised, risen) an interesting question.

12. (Rise, Raise) the picture just a few inches, please.

13. Did you (lay, lie) your jacket over the back of the chair?

14. I am sure that I (lay, laid) the folder right here.

15. The baby (taught, learned) how to walk on his first birthday.

Apply

Read each sentence. If it uses verbs correctly, write *Correct* on the line. If a verb is used incorrectly, rewrite the sentence correctly on the line.

1. My sister learned me how to ride a bike when I was five.

   _____

2. We laid in our sleeping bags and looked up at the stars.

   _____

3. The landlord says he will rise the rent next month.

   _____

4. The lawyer laid the blame on her client's sad childhood.

   _____

5. We saw the sun raise beside some pink clouds.

   _____

6. The nurse said, "Lie down on the cot and rest."

   _____

7. Mrs. Gray will teach a class on figure drawing.

   _____

8. We should lie the new area rug in the guest bedroom.

   _____

9. The custodian rises the flag every morning.

   _____

10. In this class, you will learn how to administer CPR.

    _____

11. The wedding dress had laid in the old chest for years.

    _____

12. If you raise the price, no one will buy it.

    _____

Check Up

Read each set of sentences. Then choose the sentence that uses verbs correctly.

1. A Don't raise their hopes unless you really are going to help.

    B Dan raised slowly when his alarm rang.

    C Kara is rising two children by herself.

    D The committee rose more than ten thousand dollars.

2. F Brian will learn his son to fly a kite.

    G Maria taught herself how to surf the Internet.

    H Will you learn me how to drive a car with a manual transmission?

    J Mr. Vargo is learning two classes at the junior college.

3. A Don't lay on the bed that I just made.

    B My boss just lay some contracts on my desk.

    C The tired runner fell and lay on the ground for a few minutes.

    D On summer days, I will lay in the hammock and read.

4. F When they heard the noise, the birds raised into the air.

    G On chilly nights, fog raises over open fields.

    H The sun raises in the east and sets in the west.

    J Jonah raises tomatoes and beans in his garden.

5. A Please rise your voice so I can hear you.

    B Will the merchants rise or lower their prices tomorrow?

    C Farmers rise early so they can do their morning chores.

    D Recent events have risen new problems.

6. F Pauline laid the open book on her dresser.

    G Zak laid around the house waiting for the phone to ring.

    H Kelly lay her backpack by the door last night.

    J As usual, when I laid down, the phone rang.

7. A Whoever learned Tina to swing dance did a good job.

    B When did you learn the words to that song?

    C If you'd like, I will learn you how to make a database.

    D The teacher is learning the children important safety rules.

8. F Alex found a wallet laying on the ground.

    G Phil is going to lay down until he feels better.

    H Sally laid the pictures on the table.

    J Those bags have laid beside the road for days.

Adjectives

Adjectives are words that describe a noun or a pronoun. They tell *which*, *what kind*, and *how many*.

<u>juicy</u> <u>red</u> apple   <u>second</u> chance   <u>four</u> babies

Adjectives are useful in comparing two or more objects to each other. If the adjective has just one or two syllables, add *-er* to compare two things. This is called the **comparative form.** Add *-est* to compare three or more objects. This is the **superlative form** of the adjective.

Her score was <u>lower</u> than my score.
Her score was the <u>lowest</u> in the class.

If the adjective is a longer word (two or more syllables), use *more* or *less* to compare two things. Use *most* or *least* to compare three or more things.

Lois is <u>more patient</u> than I am.
I am the <u>least patient</u> of the six of us.

Use only one adjective form in any comparison.

Incorrect: Her check is <u>more bigger</u> than mine.
Correct: Her check is <u>bigger</u> than mine.

Underline the adjectives in each sentence.

1. Did you see a small brown dog run past?

2. It's the third time I've missed the early bus.

3. The local park was littered with empty wrappers and rusty cans.

4. The new bulb seems brighter than the old one.

5. Is the home team in gray uniforms?

6. Come to an important meeting on Friday.

7. A nearby discount store claims to have the cheapest prices in town.

8. A kind passerby helped fix the flat tire.

9. What is the highest peak in the Rockies?

10. Leave wet umbrellas and muddy shoes at the door.

Practice

Adjectives may change their spelling when they are used in comparisons. Before adding -er or -est, follow these rules.

- If the adjective has one syllable, a short vowel, and a single consonant at the end, double the final consonant.

  wet　　　　　wetter (comparative)　　　wettest (superlative)

- If the adjective ends in e, drop the e.

  large　　　　larger (comparative)　　　largest (superlative)

- If the adjective ends in a consonant and y, change the y to i.

  lovely　　　　lovelier (comparative)　　　loveliest (superlative)

For a few special adjectives, change the entire word.

| good | better | best | | many | more | most |
| bad | worse | worst | | little | less | least |

Write the correct form of each adjective.

1. comparative form of sunny　　　_____

2. superlative form of good　　　_____

3. superlative form of sad　　　_____

4. comparative form of peaceful　　　_____

5. comparative form of wise　　　_____

6. superlative form of perfect　　　_____

Read each sentence. If the underlined adjective is not correct, write the proper form on the line. If there is no mistake, write *Correct*.

7. Where is the <u>most deepest</u> part of Lake Erie? _____

8. This summer is <u>more drier</u> than last summer. _____

9. She is <u>more hopeful</u> than I am about this job. _____

10. Did your cold get <u>worser</u> overnight? _____

11. What a <u>clever</u> move he made! _____

12. Hsu was the <u>more loyal</u> employee we ever hired. _____

13. Choose the <u>most prettiest</u> bouquet you can find. _____

14. There has to be a <u>more better</u> way to do this. _____

Apply

Write two adjectives to describe each noun.

1. _____ _____ tree

2. _____ _____ shirt

3. _____ _____ river

4. _____ _____ idea

Complete each sentence by writing an adjective on the line. Use the correct form for any comparisons. Do not repeat any adjective.

5. This is the _____ pizza I've ever tasted!

6. Which of the seven continents is the _____?

7. I picked _____ tomatoes from the garden.

8. Nick is _____ than Brian.

9. _____ leaves fell to the ground.

10. Is Mt. Rushmore _____ than Stone Mountain?

11. The _____ waves overturned the boat.

12. Ranelle is the _____ of the three Jefferson sisters.

Use each adjective in a sentence.

13. least expensive

_____

14. lazier

_____

15. rarest

_____

16. more playful

_____

Check Up

Read each set of sentences. Choose the sentence in which the adjective is written correctly.

1. A Chocolate ice cream is gooder than vanilla.

   B This is a good book.

   C I traded my car for a more better one.

   D He got the most good deal of all.

2. F Jamie gets more fearfuler as a storm approaches.

   G The road is more iciest than it was earlier.

   H A collie was judged the bestest dog in the show.

   J He is less confident than he was last year.

3. A Drew had a severe headache.

   B Was the pipe longest enough for the job?

   C This color is a more deeper blue than I wanted.

   D Which ocean is biggest, the Atlantic or the Pacific?

4. F My watch is even more slower than that clock!

   G The storm was most wildest during the night.

   H She is the most likely candidate for mayor.

   J I put the ice cream in the freezer to keep it more cooler.

Look at the underlined adjective in each sentence. Choose the answer that is the correct form for each underlined adjective.

5. Sal bought the <u>most popularest</u> video game on the market.

   A more popularer

   B popularest

   C most popular

   D Correct as it is

6. Please bring me the book that is <u>closest</u> to you.

   F more closer

   G most closest

   H most closer

   J Correct as it is

7. Your puppy is no <u>worser</u> than mine about chewing things.

   A badder

   B worstest

   C worse

   D Correct as it is

8. Is your friend a <u>more safer</u> driver than you are?

   F safer

   G safe

   H safest

   J Correct as it is

Adverbs

Adverbs modify (that is, change the meaning of) verbs, adjectives, or other adverbs. They often tell *when*, *how*, *where*, or *to what degree*. Sometimes they add a positive or negative sense to the words they modify. Many adverbs end in *-ly*.

> The gentle rain fell lightly on my very warm face.
> (*lightly* tells *how*; *very* tells *how much*)

> No, I will not attend the meeting tomorrow.
> (*no* and *not* are negatives; *tomorrow* tells *when*)

Adverbs change form in comparisons in the same way that adjectives do. For short adverbs of one or two syllables, add *-er* to compare two things. For longer adverbs, use *more* or *less* for the comparative form.

For short adverbs, add *-est* to compare three or more objects. For longer adverbs, use *most* or *least* for the superlative form. Use just one form of the adverb in any comparison.

> **Incorrect:** My mail came more earlier yesterday than it did today.
> **Correct:** My mail came earlier yesterday than it did today.

Underline the adverb in each sentence.

1. Was your dog barking noisily all night?

2. Go to the bank now before it closes.

3. Gary never remembers to bring his lunch.

4. Sounds echo more loudly in an empty room than in a crowded one.

5. Nina boldly drew several lines on the blank paper.

6. A flock of sparrows quickly ate the birdseed I had scattered.

7. Alma sings most clearly of all the choir members.

8. Did you purchase that car recently?

9. Yes, I returned the book to the library.

10. Dante exercises less vigorously than I do.

11. We almost missed the last bus.

12. They searched carefully for the missing papers.

Practice

Follow these rules before adding *-er* or *-est* to an adverb:

- If the adverb has one syllable, a short vowel, and a single consonant at the end, double the final consonant.
- If the adverb ends in *e*, drop the *e*. (*late, later*)
- If the adverb ends in a consonant and *y*, change the *y* to *i*. (*steady, steadier*)

A few adverbs have a special form for comparisons.

well	better	best		much	more	most
badly	worse	worst		little	less	least

Fill in the chart below with the correct adverbs.

Adverb	Comparative Form	Superlative Form
1.	more roughly	2.
soon	3.	4.
5.	worse	6.
7.	8.	most neatly
early	9.	10.

Read each sentence. If the form of the underlined adverb is not correct, write the proper form on the line. If the form is correct, write *Correct*.

11. Of the six singers at the tryouts, the first one sang <u>more sweetly</u>. _____

12. The ground shook <u>violently</u> during the earthquake. _____

13. We crossed the flooded street <u>most safely</u>. _____

14. Jan skates <u>more better</u> than I do. _____

15. Of the two fans, the gold one works <u>most quietly</u>. _____

16. We <u>closely</u> followed our guide through the museum. _____

17. Jack threw <u>most farthest</u> in the pitching contest. _____

18. Nobody complains <u>more loudly</u> than Jeremy. _____

Apply

Rewrite each sentence, adding at least one adverb to describe the verb, an adjective, or another adverb.

1. The little boy swims fearlessly.

   _____

2. Some wealthy people buy expensive boats.

   _____

3. The red car turned the corner.

   _____

4. My neighbors lost their friendly dog.

   _____

Read each pair of sentences. Choose the sentence in which the correct form of the adverb is used.

5. **A** We are most deeply involved in the project than you are.

   B We are more deeply involved in the project than you are.

6. **A** Does the bus or the train leave earliest in the morning?

   B Does the bus or the train leave earlier in the morning?

7. **A** Vic talks faster than anyone else I know.

   B Vic talks more faster than anyone else I know.

8. **A** Ann speaks French the most fluently of all the members of her family.

   B Ann speaks French the more fluently of all the members of her family.

9. **A** The linebacker pushed harder than he should have.

   B The linebacker pushed more harder than he should have.

10. **A** James thought he was treated less fairly than I had been.

    B James thought he was treated least fairly than I had been.

Adverbs **63**

Check Up

Look at the underlined word or words in each sentence. Choose the answer that is written correctly for the underlined part.

1. Our hand soap cleans more better than the leading brand.

   A gooder

   B better

   C best

   D Correct as it is

2. The veteran marched proudly in the Memorial Day parade.

   F proud

   G more proudly

   H proudest

   J Correct as it is

3. Which member of the relay team runs more faster of all?

   A fastest

   B more fast

   C faster

   D Correct as it is

4. In the traffic accident, Joe was hurt more badly than the other driver.

   F most badly

   G worse

   H worst

   J Correct as it is

5. I watch TV rarelier than most people do.

   A most rarely

   B rare

   C more rarely

   D Correct as it is

6. This gasoline makes your car run more efficiently than ever.

   F most efficiently

   G efficiently

   H efficient

   J Correct as it is

7. The bus more suddenly screeched to a stop.

   A suddener

   B most suddenly

   C suddenly

   D Correct as it is

8. Some problems must be corrected most immediately than others.

   F more immediately

   G immediately

   H immediate

   J Correct as it is

Adjective or Adverb?

Both adjectives and adverbs are modifiers. They limit or change the meaning of the words they modify. Some words can be used as either adjectives or adverbs. Many more words that act as adjectives can be changed to adverbs simply by adding *-ly*. A few words fit both categories.

> Drive in the slow lane. (adjective, tells *what kind*)
> Go slow. Drive slowly. (adverbs, tell *how*)

Because adjectives and adverbs are so similar, it is important to know how they differ. Adjectives describe only nouns and pronouns. They tell *which*, *what kind*, or *how many*. Adverbs describe verbs, adjectives, or other adverbs. They tell *how*, *when*, *where*, or *to what degree*. Many adverbs, but not all, end in *-ly*.

Look at the underlined word in each sentence. If it is an adjective, write ADJ on the line. If it is an adverb, write ADV.

1. Three clients are speaking at the meeting.   _____

2. Enroll now and save money!   _____

3. The usher cheerfully showed us to our seats.   _____

4. Because of heavy traffic, Ben nearly missed his flight.   _____

5. Do you usually come this way?   _____

6. This is a lovely portrait of your family.   _____

7. Which store advertises the very lowest prices in town?   _____

8. I bought a new car yesterday.   _____

9. Video Barn carries a large selection of CDs.   _____

10. She is most likely to be elected president.   _____

11. Your homemade ice cream is fabulous.   _____

12. Take the scenic route if you have the time.   _____

Practice

Adding *-ly* to an adjective that describes *what kind* changes the word to an adverb that describes *how*. Here are a few examples:

Adjective	Adverb
soft	softly
brave	bravely
easy	easily

Notice the difference between adjectives and adverbs when they are used in comparisons.

Adjective	Adverb
soft, softer, softest	softly, more softly, most softly
brave, braver, bravest	bravely, more bravely, most bravely
easy, easier, easiest	easily, more easily, most easily

A few special adjectives and adverbs have the same form in comparisons.

Adjective:	good	better	best		bad	worse	worst
Adverb:	well	better	best		badly	worse	worst

Read each sentence and determine which word is being modified. Circle the word being modified and underline the correct modifier, either adjective or adverb.

1. Which one has a (more sweetly, sweeter) taste, molasses or honey?

2. The impatient driver glared (angrily, angry) at the slow truck before him.

3. This is a (good, well) recipe for salsa.

4. Use the (widest, most widely) paintbrush you have for that job.

5. Of all the varieties of roses, which one is (most beautiful, most beautifully)?

6. He plays golf very (bad, badly).

7. You are (more clever, more cleverly) at solving puzzles than I am.

8. Is the water in the pool (more warmly, warmer) than the lake?

9. Your fudge is the (smoothest, most smoothly) I've ever tasted!

10. Rover barked (continuous, continuously) in obedience class.

11. We (near, nearly) fell on the icy sidewalk.

12. What animal moves (most silently, most silent) through the jungle?

Apply

Read each set of sentences. Use either the adjective or adverb to complete each sentence. Change the word to its comparative or superlative form if necessary.

1. wet   wetly

    A This is the _____ spring in 50 years.

    B The tree branch smacked _____ against my face.

    C The ground seems _____ in this spot than over there.

2. firm   firmly

    F Dave spoke _____ to the unruly child.

    G This is the _____ mattress I've ever slept on.

    H She gripped the wheel _____ than she had done earlier.

3. restful   restfully

    A This ad claims that a train trip is _____ than a bus tour.

    B Did you sleep _____ last night than you did the previous night?

    C What a _____ day this has been!

4. daring   daringly

    F Of the three gymnasts, Mandy moved _____ on the balance beam.

    G No pilot was _____ than Major Anderson was.

    H At first, only a few women were _____ enough to wear bloomers.

Write an adjective or an adverb to complete each sentence. Use the correct form for any comparison.

5. A steak is _____ than a hamburger.

6. The faucet dripped _____ all night long.

7. The second sled glided _____ down the track than the other sleds.

8. Drive _____ through the construction zone.

9. What is the _____ mountain in North America?

Check Up

Read each group of sentences. Choose the sentence in which the adverb or adjective is written correctly.

1. **A** This is the prettiest bouquet in the flower shop.

   B Yesterday was more icily than today.

   C She honest stated her opinion to us.

   D Was the house built on a solidly foundation?

2. **F** He easiliest made the catch.

   G The couple swayed to the music most graceful.

   H We were hopelessly lost in the vast museum.

   J She sighed unhappier.

3. **A** This rapidly pace is too much for me.

   B The river is more shallowly than usual.

   C Last summer was the driest on record.

   D Phil spoke calmest to the group.

4. **F** After swimming far from shore, the boy called weak for help.

   G She acted braver than her sister did.

   H Al reads more fluent than he did last year.

   J Dad gently laid my baby in her crib.

Read each sentence and look at the underlined word or words. Choose the answer that is written correctly for each underlined part.

5. Which of these two pictures is <u>more darkly</u>?

   A most darkly

   B darker

   C darkly

   D Correct as it is

6. It was the <u>happily</u> moment of my life!

   F most happily

   G happiest

   H more happily

   J Correct as it is

7. The referee judged the game <u>fairly</u>.

   A fair

   B fairer

   C fairest

   D Correct as it is

8. Were you treated <u>more helpful</u> than I was?

   F most helpful

   G helpfully

   H more helpfully

   J Correct as it is

Using Negative Words Correctly

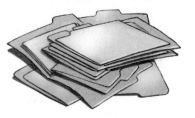

Two negative words in the same clause or sentence are often referred to as a **double negative**. In formal or business situations, double negatives should be avoided.

Contractions that end in *n't* are negative words, and so are the words *hardly*, *scarcely*, and *barely*. Here are some other common negative words:

never	no	none	not
nothing	nobody	no one	nowhere

To correct a double negative, remove one of the negative words.

Double negative:	Keith couldn't find the folders nowhere.
Standard:	Keith couldn't find the folders anywhere.
Standard:	Keith could find the folders nowhere.

Circle the double negatives in each sentence. If the sentence does not have a double negative, write *Correct* on the line.

1. The secretary doesn't see no mistakes in the letter. _____

2. The workers don't hardly know where to begin. _____

3. I wasn't asking for any special favors. _____

4. Didn't no one look at a map before we got into the car? _____

5. Ellen didn't ever expect to be elected club president. _____

6. Our neighbors haven't said nothing to us about building a fence. _____

7. Doesn't nobody want to see that horror movie with me? _____

8. I don't want to go nowhere until this storm ends. _____

9. My children can't hardly get to see their grandparents anymore. _____

10. The waiter offered Shaylah black pepper, but she didn't want none. _____

Practice

Circle the word that completes each sentence correctly.

1. I couldn't (never, ever) give a speech to a crowd of people.

2. The thief stole the necklace when no one (was, wasn't) looking.

3. Didn't (nothing, anything) addressed to me come in today's mail?

4. Mom offered me some spaghetti, but I couldn't eat (none, any).

5. Kevin hasn't been (anywhere, nowhere) east of the Mississippi River.

6. Tess couldn't read (none, any) of the fine print at the bottom of the coupon.

7. I wouldn't want (anyone, no one) else to be my maid of honor.

8. We knew Carrie was sick when she didn't want (anything, nothing) for dinner.

9. Bill never had (no, any) interest in skydiving until now.

10. There (were, weren't) scarcely enough doughnuts for everyone to have one.

Read the paragraph and look at the numbered, underlined parts. Choose the answer that is written correctly for each underlined part.

        Fire safety is of primary importance when you are camping. Clearly,
(11)   no one wants to see no flames destroying the beauty of our forests. When
(12)   you enjoy a campfire, don't take no chances. Stay by the fire at all times.
(13)   When you go to bed, never leave no embers burning. Douse them with
(14)   water and make sure they aren't hardly touching one another. If
(15)   no one never breaks these simple rules, we will all enjoy our forests for many
     years.

11. **A** no one hardly wants to see flames

     B no one wants to see flames

     C no one never wants to see flames

12. **F** don't take any chances

     G never take no chances

     H don't never take no chances

13. **A** you shouldn't leave barely any

     B don't never leave any

     C never leave any

14. **F** they don't hardly touch

     G they are not never touching

     H they aren't touching

15. **A** we never break

     B we don't hardly break

     C no one doesn't break

Apply

Read each sentence. If it contains a double negative, rewrite it correctly on the line. If it uses negative words correctly, write *Correct*.

1. Moira's car won't never start on cold mornings.

   _____

2. I didn't hardly have time to relax before I had to cook dinner.

   _____

3. I don't want none of you to worry about me.

   _____

4. Won't this speaker ever get to the point?

   _____

5. My cat doesn't jump onto the furniture no more.

   _____

6. Erika didn't want nothing to spoil her perfect evening.

   _____

7. Don't let no one in while I am away.

   _____

8. Nancy never wants no mushrooms on her pizza.

   _____

9. We haven't gone anywhere together in a long time.

   _____

10. Lamar never has no time to watch TV anymore.

    _____

Check Up

Read each set of sentences. Choose the sentence that uses negative words correctly.

1. **A** Wendy couldn't understand none of the pilot's words.

   B No one could teach that dog no tricks.

   C Doesn't anybody have some change for the parking meter?

   D I don't have nothing more to say to you.

2. **F** Tony couldn't find anything on the menu that he wanted.

   G I can't never find the Big Dipper in the sky.

   H Jake doesn't go nowhere without his wallet.

   J Lauren wouldn't let nobody give her a loan.

3. **A** There wasn't no lifeguard on duty that night.

   B I couldn't eat no more pie right now.

   C Aunt Jean didn't ever forget our birthdays.

   D One storm wasn't scarcely over before the next one began.

4. **F** I can't never get my checking account to balance.

   G Pat can't find none of the pencils she just bought.

   H There isn't nothing I like better than a walk by the ocean.

   J Today's forecast doesn't say anything about rain.

Read each sentence and look at the underlined words. Choose the answer that is written correctly for the underlined words.

5. You can't hardly expect me to remember everything.

   A can't never expect

   B can hardly expect

   C can't scarcely expect

   D Correct as it is

6. Matt hasn't never taken any classes in computer science.

   F has never taken no

   G hasn't never taken no

   H hasn't ever taken any

   J Correct as it is

7. Mike won't let anything distract him from his job.

   A won't let nothing

   B won't hardly let anything

   C never lets nothing

   D Correct as it is

8. Adam never shares none of his lunch with his friends.

   F never shares any

   G doesn't share none

   H doesn't never share any

   J Correct as it is

Review

Nouns

Nouns name persons, places, or things. A singular noun names one, and a plural noun names more than one. **Common nouns** name any person, place, or thing. **Proper nouns** name particular persons, places, and things. Every word in a proper noun should be capitalized.

Pronouns

Pronouns are words used in place of nouns. Pronouns should agree with their antecedents in number, gender, and person. Some types of pronouns include *personal*, *relative*, and *reflexive*.

Verbs

Verbs name actions or states of being. Verbs are classified as **action verbs, linking verbs,** or **helping verbs.**

The form of a verb changes to show the time of its action. These different forms are called **tenses**. *Simple* and *perfect* are two verb tenses. Every verb must agree with its subject in number.

Certain verb pairs (*rise, raise*; *lie, lay*; *teach, learn*) can be confusing. Take special care to use them correctly.

Adjectives and Adverbs

Adjectives describe nouns or pronouns or limit them in some way. They tell *which, what kind*, or *how many*. **Adverbs** modify verbs, adjectives, and other adverbs. They tell *how, when, where*, or *to what degree*. Adjectives and adverbs change their forms when they are used to compare things or actions.

Negative Words

Do not use two negative words in the same clause or sentence. Negative words include the following: *no, not, never, hardly, scarcely, barely,* and all contractions made using the word *not*.

Assessment

Choose the word that correctly completes each sentence.

1. When _____ came to this country, I was six years old.

   A we

   B them

   C me

   D your

2. If we want the bedroom painted, we must do it _____.

   F themselves

   G myself

   H ourself

   J ourselves

3. The artists _____ created the mural used unusual colors.

   A that

   B whom

   C whose

   D who

4. The train _____ on Track 14.

   F have arrived

   G arrive

   H is arriving

   J arriving

5. Next June, my parents _____ their fiftieth wedding anniversary.

   A will celebrate

   B have celebrated

   C celebrating

   D celebrated

6. Some medicines in the bathroom cabinet _____.

   F has expired

   G was expired

   H have expired

   J expires

7. The club _____ money to help families in need.

   A rises

   B raises

   C has risen

   D rised

8. Please speak _____ when you are talking to adults.

   F politer

   G more politely

   H more politer

   J most politest

9. That cereal is _____ than a cookie.

   A sweetly

   B sweet

   C sweeter

   D more sweetly

10. Ginny watched _____ as her daughter played the violin solo.

    F most proudest

    G proud

    H prouder

    J proudly

Assessment continued

Read each set of sentences. Choose the sentence that is written correctly.

11. A I am trying to see who just rang the doorbell.

  B Tonight, we will seen the new horror flick.

  C Roy has ate the last cookie from the cookie jar.

  D Trash and litter was left behind after the rock concert.

12. F Don couldn't hardly think of what to write on the card.

  G Phyllis hadn't never gone camping before last weekend.

  H Robin couldn't see anything clearly using the binoculars.

  J I hope this job won't be nothing like my last one.

13. A The nurses and the doctor reports that Mom is feeling better.

  B A cold and a cough is keeping me out of work this week.

  C Muffins or a coffeecake makes a nice breakfast treat.

  D My dogs and my neighbor's dog disturbs my sleep every night.

14. F Which of these black suitcases is your?

  G When the house is mine, I will take down those dead trees.

  H You told I that joke several times before.

  J The manager hisself argued with the umpire.

15. A I am never seen such a tall tree before.

  B Americans has been enjoying their forests for centuries.

  C Many old trees have been cut down for their lumber.

  D When we has destroyed the trees, what will happen to forest animals?

16. F The most easiest solution is often the best one.

  G I'm afraid that the problem is now worse than before.

  H I will plant the fern in the shadier spot in the whole yard.

  J Van can see more better with his new glasses.

17. A You can solve this simply math problem if you concentrate.

  B Of all my students, she wrote her name most legible.

  C The secretary's phone rang constant all day.

  D The runner gratefully accepted a bottle of water.

18. F I'm sure I lay my keys on this table.

  G If you lie quietly, you can hear the sound of the waves.

  H Gabrielle laid on the sofa and watched TV.

  J Mary has lain a blanket over her sleeping son.

Assessment continued

Read the paragraphs and look at the numbered, underlined parts. Choose the answer that is written correctly for each underlined part.

        A few days ago, I tried to teach my younger sister Lynn how to drive.
(19)   What a mistake! I thought that there was no one <u>more sweetly</u> than Lynn,
        but when she got behind the wheel, she was downright scary! She thought
(20)   she knew everything. There <u>wasn't nothing</u> I could do or say that she
(21)   would take seriously. If I <u>am asked</u> her to turn right, she would turn left.
(22)   If I told her to slow down, she would speed up. Maybe <u>her</u> will listen
        more closely to a teacher from the local driving school.

19. **A** sweetest

     B sweeter

     C sweetlier

     D Correct as it is

20. **F** wasn't hardly anything

     G was never nothing

     H was nothing

     J Correct as it is

21. **A** asked

     B will be asking

     C will ask

     D Correct as it is

22. **F** he

     G hers

     H she

     J Correct as it is

(23)   There <u>isn't nothing</u> more relaxing than tubing down a lazy river. What
(24)   is tubing? It's probably the <u>least strenuously</u> sport possible. To tube, all
        you do is sit in an old inner tube and let a river carry you downstream.
(25)   While people in canoes work hard paddling, you just <u>be watching</u> the
(26)   clouds go by. Next summer, go tubing! You <u>will have</u> a great time.

23. **A** is nothing

     B wasn't nothing

     C is scarcely nothing

     D Correct as it is

24. **F** less strenuous

     G strenuously

     H least strenuous

     J Correct as it is

25. **A** has been watching

     B am watching

     C watch

     D Correct as it is

26. **F** were had

     G is having

     H has had

     J Correct as it is

Complete Sentences and Fragments

Complete sentences are important for clear speech and writing. A complete sentence has both a subject and a predicate. The **subject** names the person or thing that is doing something. The **predicate** tells what the subject is doing. The predicate always includes a verb.

The salesman | opened his briefcase.
  subject   predicate (verb is underlined)

Here are two common types of sentence fragments and a way to correct each one:

1. If the fragment has a subject but no predicate, add a predicate.

   Fragment: The cows in the pasture.
   Complete sentence: The cows in the pasture eat grass.

2. If the fragment has a predicate but no subject, add a subject.

   Fragment: Danced until one in the morning.
   Complete sentence: Bruce and Lena danced until one in the morning.

Write *CS* beside each complete sentence. Underline its subject and circle its predicate. Write *F* beside each fragment.

1. _____ A dancer on the stage.

2. _____ Climbed to the top of the maple tree.

3. _____ Leonard didn't buy the motorcycle.

4. _____ Three seats in the front row.

5. _____ The painting is in a gold frame.

6. _____ Lily's favorite cousin.

7. _____ Is not accepting applications this week.

8. _____ Ran down Main Street with a bunch of roses.

9. _____ Harry mowed the lawn yesterday.

10. _____ Lucia's apartment is on the fifth floor.

Practice

Now look at two more types of sentence fragments and ways to correct them.

3. The fragment is a phrase with no subject or predicate. One way to correct this is to add a subject and predicate. However, the fragment may actually be part of the sentence next to it.

   Fragment: Brad parked the car. Behind the hardware store.

   Complete sentence: Brad parked the car behind the hardware store. (Add the fragment to the sentence before it.)

4. The fragment is a subordinate clause. At first glance, a subordinate clause may seem to be a sentence. Like a sentence, it has a subject and a predicate. But a subordinate clause does not make sense by itself. A subordinate clause begins with words such as *after, although, as, because, if, since, though, unless, when, where,* and *while.* This kind of fragment usually belongs with the sentence before or after it.

   Fragment: Alan ordered a pizza. Although he's on a diet.

   Complete sentence: Alan ordered pizza although he's on a diet. (Add the fragment to the sentence before it.)

Write *CS* beside each complete sentence. Beside each phrase fragment, write *Phrase*. Beside each clause fragment, write *Clause*.

1. _____ Emily wrote a long letter.

2. _____ Because his legs are too long.

3. _____ If nobody else wants one.

4. _____ Under the floorboards.

5. _____ She borrowed her mother's white dress.

6. _____ Hidden beneath a stack of papers.

7. _____ Since they went to Las Vegas.

8. _____ Paul plays the lottery every day.

9. _____ They caught a record number of fish.

10. _____ Ernesto and his grandfather.

Apply

Correct each of the following sentence fragments. Write the complete sentence on the line.

1. Told the story about the Grand Canyon.

   _____

2. Since her trip to Mexico. Cathy has been taking salsa dance lessons.

   _____

3. We coasted to the gas station. With the tank on empty.

   _____

4. Changed the tire on the side of the road.

   _____

5. Rita and Fred's brand new RV camper.

   _____

6. Lisa brought a map. In case we lose our way.

   _____

7. Going to visit Deborah and Wally.

   _____

8. Because Natalie is the oldest. The other kids listen to her.

   _____

9. Ran around the track five times.

   _____

10. The cars in this lane.

   _____

Check Up

Read each set of sentences. Then choose the complete sentence.

1. A Needs a shovel and a pitchfork.
    B The pumpkins glow on the porch.
    C A big glass of apple cider.
    D Because we don't have any sugar left.

2. F Nan's restaurant opens at six o'clock.
    G Had a T-bone steak for dinner.
    H A set of silverware rolled in a napkin.
    J Lorenzo and his older brother.

3. A Although she knew I'd be late.
    B It always snows on Elaine's birthday.
    C Neil's old pair of boxing gloves.
    D Went to Georgia last week.

4. F Played her saxophone on the fire escape.
    G The cookies with chocolate stripes.
    H And then ordered more dessert.
    J Kathryn plays the piano beautifully.

Read the paragraph and look at its underlined parts. Choose the answer that is written correctly for each underlined part.

(5)   When the TV series *The Simpsons* premiered in 1990. No cartoon had been seen on prime time for twenty years. It was a risky project for creator Matt Groening. Since then, *The Simpsons* has become one of TV's most popular shows.
(6)   More than 60 million people. Watch the show every week.

5. A When the TV series *The Simpsons* premiered. In 1990 no cartoon had been seen in prime time for twenty years.
    B When the TV series *The Simpsons* premiered in 1990, no cartoon had been seen in prime time for twenty years.
    C When the TV series *The Simpsons* premiered in 1990 no cartoon. Had been seen in prime time for twenty years.
    D Correct as it is

6. F More than 60 million. People watch the show every week.
    G More than 60 million people, watch the show every week.
    H More than 60 million people watch the show every week.
    J Correct as it is

Run-On Sentences

Avoid run-on sentences when you write. **Run-on sentences** combine two or more sentences without the proper punctuation. Run-ons make it hard for readers to know where one idea ends and the next begins.

In many run-on sentences, two sentences are joined with no punctuation between them. In the following run-on sentence, the first sentence is underlined.

Kim loves traveling she wants to visit Italy this fall.

In other run-ons, two sentences are joined with just a comma.

Kim loves traveling, she wants to visit Italy this fall.

Draw a vertical line between the first sentence and the second sentence in the following run-on sentences.

1. The Cotton Club is downtown, they have live music on Saturdays.

2. We went to the beach the kids love to swim.

3. Don cleaned out the cupboard, he found his army knife in there.

4. Scott broke the VCR, he's trying to fix it himself.

5. Warren is a great cook his wife is lucky.

6. Ellen went home she lives in Chicago.

7. They're charging three dollars for a soda, I don't think I'm thirsty.

8. She plays softball, he runs five miles a day.

Write *CS* beside each complete sentence and *RO* beside each run-on sentence.

9. _____ The library is closed but will reopen tomorrow.

10. _____ The history section is upstairs take the elevator and turn left.

11. _____ Lucy and Carmen live near Central Park.

12. _____ These biscuits taste good Nancy uses lots of butter.

13. _____ Rafael is from Colombia he just arrived last week.

14. _____ Her favorite restaurant is in Brooklyn it's called Sopa.

Practice

To correct a run-on, use one of the following methods. Choose the best method for each situation.

1. Split the sentence in two. Add an end mark to the first sentence. Begin the second sentence with a capital letter.

   Kim loves traveling. She will visit Italy this fall.

2. Insert a comma after the first statement, and add a conjunction such as *and, but,* or *or* after the comma.

   Kim loves traveling, and she will visit Italy this fall.

3. Insert a semicolon after the first statement. Do not capitalize the first word of the second statement.

   Kim loves traveling; she will visit Italy this fall.

4. After the first statement, insert a semicolon and a transition word such as *however, nevertheless,* or *therefore,* followed by a comma.

   Kim loves traveling; therefore, she will visit Italy this fall.

Read each run-on sentence. Then read the pair of sentences beneath it. Choose the sentence that corrects the run-on sentence.

1. The snowstorm delayed some flights my plane came in one hour late.
   A The snowstorm delayed some flights, my plane came in one hour late.
   B The snowstorm delayed some flights; my plane came in one hour late.

2. I like the red dress better the blue one is much less expensive.
   A I like the red dress better the blue one; is much less expensive.
   B I like the red dress better; however, the blue one is much less expensive.

3. This goldfish has a big belly do you think it's pregnant?
   A This goldfish has a big belly. Do you think it's pregnant?
   B This goldfish has a big belly, do you think it's pregnant?

4. Our town's newspaper was started in 1890 it's still being published.
   A Our town's newspaper was started in 1890, it's still being published
   B Our town's newspaper was started in 1890, and it's still being published.

5. Al loves to bowl he has his own bowling ball and shoes.
   A Al loves to bowl; he has his own bowling ball and shoes.
   B Al loves to bowl, he has his own bowling ball and shoes.

Apply

Decide if each item is a complete sentence or a run-on. If it is a complete sentence, write *CS* on the line. If it is a run-on, correct it.

1. Lea and Ed have known each other for five years; they got married last fall.

   _____

2. Dana has to leave work early, she has a dental appointment.

   _____

3. The Ferris wheel is fun I like the roller coaster better.

   _____

4. Jonathan grew up in a small town in Mississippi.

   _____

5. Teresa had to go home and change, her shirt was stained with motor oil.

   _____

6. Victor knew that the pasta was overcooked nevertheless he took a giant helping.

   _____

7. Laura told us that she was related to the royal family, and we believed her!

   _____

8. My neighbor plays the piano; sometimes I hear him practicing.

   _____

9. The newspaper costs fifty cents can I borrow a dime?

   _____

10. These shoes are too tight, they're giving me blisters.

    _____

Check Up

Read each group of sentences. Then choose the complete sentence.

1. **A** Aisha moved to New York, she lives on the Lower East Side.

   B Tony and Sal ordered lobster; they love seafood.

   C I'll call Tim he should be invited.

   D I'd like to stay for dessert, I have to go home.

2. **F** There is too much traffic on the highway let's take back roads.

   G Joy's brother is a plumber, you should call him.

   H Charlotte did all of the electrical wiring herself.

   J Rick's grandfather still calls bingo; every Friday night.

3. **A** I'll buy the telephone; however, I don't want the extra-long cord.

   B Mickey has a jigsaw, he'll let you borrow it.

   C I can't reach the light I need a stepladder.

   D Cassie had said that the play was bad, nevertheless we went to see it.

4. **F** Brad and Janet had a yard sale, they made over $200.

   G Everyone in my family loves olives, but I can't stand them.

   H Cindy planted tomatoes she thinks they'll be ready to harvest soon.

   J It snowed last night the roads are still icy.

Read the paragraph and look at the underlined sections. Choose the answer that is written correctly for each underlined section.

The city of Savannah, Georgia, was designed by James Oglethorpe in 1733. Its streets, based on Roman plans, are
(5) laid out with squares. There are 21 squares each is unique.
(6) Cars have to drive around the squares, this keeps traffic slow in downtown Savannah. City residents enjoy the shade trees, the park benches, and the peaceful atmosphere.

5. **A** There are 21 squares, each is unique.

   B There are 21 squares, and each is unique.

   C There, are 21 squares each is unique.

   D Correct as it is

6. **F** Cars have to drive around the squares this keeps traffic slow; in downtown Savannah.

   G Cars have to drive around the squares this keeps. Traffic slow in downtown Savannah.

   H Cars have to drive around the squares; this keeps traffic slow in downtown Savannah.

   J Correct as it is

Sentence Combining: Compound Sentence Parts

You can combine sentences that have common parts. In the first example, two sentences with the same predicate are combined.

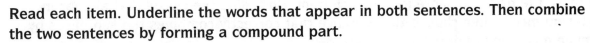

Casey <u>ate lunch</u>. Ted <u>ate lunch</u>.

Casey and Ted ate lunch.

The sentence that is formed has a compound subject.

In the second example, two sentences with the same subject are combined.

<u>Martin</u> went to the store. <u>He</u> rented a video.

Martin went to the store and rented a video.

This time, the sentence that is formed has a compound predicate.

Read each item. Underline the words that appear in both sentences. Then combine the two sentences by forming a compound part.

1. Thunder scares my dog. Lightning scares my dog.

   _____

2. Jian plays violin. Jian tutors music students.

   _____

3. Mr. Silva witnessed the accident. His son witnessed the accident.

   _____

4. Ice cream sundaes are loaded with calories. Chocolate cakes are loaded with calories.

   _____

5. The band performed its hit songs. The band thrilled the audience.

   _____

6. Alex jacked up the car. Alex changed the flat tire.

   _____

Practice

You can combine sentences by forming compound subjects and predicates. You can also combine sentences by forming other compound parts. Here are some examples:

<u>Del ordered</u> five boxes of pens.

<u>Del ordered</u> ten pads of paper.

Del ordered five boxes of pens and ten pads of paper.

<u>Mrs. Costas teaches</u> geometry classes.

<u>Mrs. Costas teaches</u> algebra classes.

Mrs. Costa teaches geometry and algebra classes.

Sentences with related topics may be joined even when there is no repetition in them.

The steps are slippery. You can hold the railing.

The steps are slippery, but you can hold the railing.

Compare the first two sentences in each item. Underline the words that appear in both sentences. Then choose the sentence that correctly combines the sentences by forming a compound part.

1. The actor has starred in films. The actor has starred in Broadway shows.

   A The actor has starred in films and Broadway shows.

   B The actor has starred in films and has starred in Broadway shows.

2. The magazine article is interesting. The magazine article is informative.

   A The magazine article is interesting and it's informative, too.

   B The magazine article is interesting and informative.

3. Carla pays her insurance bills early. Carla pays her credit card bills early.

   A Carla pays her insurance bills and credit cards early.

   B Carla pays her insurance and credit card bills early.

4. Ms. Kerr praised the stage crew. Ms. Kerr praised the cast.

   A Ms. Kerr praised the stage crew and praised the cast.

   B Ms. Kerr praised the stage crew and cast.

5. We bought fresh tomatoes at the farmers' market. We bought fresh corn at the farmers' market.

   A We bought fresh tomatoes and corn at the farmers' market.

   B We bought fresh tomatoes and fresh corn and at the farmers' market.

Apply

Read the underlined sentences. Decide whether the final sentence combines the underlined ones correctly. If it does, write *Correct*. If it does not, rewrite the combined sentence correctly.

1. Will you please pass the salt?

    Will you please pass the pepper?

    Will you please pass the salt, and will you please pass the pepper?

    _____

2. The passengers returned their seats to an upright position.

    The passengers buckled their seat belts.

    The passengers returned their seats to an upright position and buckled their seat belts.

    _____

3. Bears hibernate in the winter.

    Ground squirrels hibernate in the winter.

    Bears hibernate and ground squirrels in the winter.

    _____

4. Paul baked some delicious cookies.

    Liz baked some delicious cookies.

    Paul baked some delicious cookies, and Liz baked some delicious cookies.

    _____

5. Kristen filed the receipts for the week.

    Kristen filed the orders for the week.

    Kristen filed the receipts for the week and the orders.

    _____

6. The security guard at the airport inspected the suitcases.

    The security guard at the airport inspected the backpacks.

    The security guard inspected the suitcases at the airport and the backpacks.

    _____

Check Up

Read each set of underlined sentences. Then choose the sentence that correctly combines the underlined sentences.

1. The tornado damaged the city hall.

   The tornado damaged many houses.

   A The tornado damaged the city hall and damaged many houses.

   B The tornado damaged the city hall and many houses.

   C The tornado damaged the city hall, and it damaged many houses.

   D When the tornado damaged the city hall, it damaged many houses, too.

2. Our CDs are stacked on the shelf.

   Our tapes are stacked on the shelf.

   F Our CDs are stacked on the shelf and with the tapes.

   G Our CDs are stacked and the tapes are stacked on the shelf.

   H Our CDs and tapes are stacked on the shelf.

   J Our CDs are stacked on the shelf, and the tapes are stacked.

3. Tom started taking the new medicine.

   Tom felt better right away.

   A Tom started taking the new medicine, so he would feel better right away.

   B Before Tom started taking the new medicine, he felt better right away.

   C Tom started taking the new medicine, and he felt better right away.

   D Tom started taking the new medicine and felt better right away.

4. Mr. Blaine addressed the letters and packages.

   He mailed the letters.

   He mailed the packages.

   F Mr. Blaine addressed the letters and packages and mailed the letters, and then he mailed the packages.

   G Mr. Blaine addressed the letters and packages and mailed them.

   H Mr. Blaine addressed the letters and mailed the packages.

   J Mr. Blaine addressed and mailed the letters and packages.

Sentence Combining: Adding Modifiers

Adjectives and adjective phrases give details about persons, places, and things. Adding these modifiers makes your writing more interesting. However, avoid using a second sentence just to include a modifier. Combine the sentences instead. Place an adjective before the noun it modifies. Place an adjective phrase after the noun it modifies.

Here are some examples of combining sentences to add modifiers:

Adding an adjective:

Neil built a <u>shed</u> for his tools.

The shed was <u>large</u>.

Neil built a <u>large shed</u> for his tools.

Adding an adjective phrase:

These <u>boots</u> are too small for me.

The boots are <u>in my closet</u>.

These <u>boots in my closet</u> are too small for me.

Read each pair of sentences. In the second sentence, underline the noun that is modified. Underline the same noun in the first sentence. Then combine the sentences, adding the modifier to the first sentence.

1. Ralph's car stopped in the middle of the street. His car is old.

    _____

2. As a hobby, the Greenes collect masks. The masks are from Africa.

    _____

3. The manager gave a bonus to each worker. The bonus was small.

    _____

4. That opal ring is beautiful. The ring is in the jewelry case.

    _____

5. Leslie rented a summer cottage. The cottage is near the lake.

    _____

Practice

Adding adverbs and adverb phrases can improve and strengthen your writing. Adverbs modify verbs, telling *how, when, where,* and *why* an action occurs. They also modify adjectives or other adverbs. When possible, place an adverb or adverb phrase in the same sentence as the word it modifies.

Adding an adverb:

My daughter opened her birthday present.

She did so eagerly.

My daughter eagerly opened her birthday present.

Adding an adverb phrase:

Hank hauls building materials.

He takes them to the new mall.

Hank hauls building materials to the new mall.

Each sentence in Column B combines one of the sentence pairs in Column A. On the line in Column A, write the number of the matching sentence in Column B.

Column A

1. The quarterback clutched the football. He held the ball tightly.

   _____

2. Jets landed at the busy airport. They came in every ten minutes. _____

3. Clarice delivers packages and mail. She travels throughout the city.

   _____

4. We read the architect's blueprints. We did this before we started the job.

   _____

5. Emilio removed the old paint from the chair. He worked swiftly. _____

6. A wall surrounded the ancient city. The wall was very high. _____

Column B

A Emilio swiftly removed the old paint from the chair.

B We read the architect's blueprints before we started the job.

C Jets landed at the busy airport every ten minutes.

D The quarterback tightly clutched the football.

E Clarice delivers packages and mail throughout the city.

F A very high wall surrounded the ancient city.

Apply

Read each set of underlined sentences. Decide whether the final sentence combines the underlined ones correctly. If it does, write *Correct*. If it does not, rewrite the combined sentence correctly.

1. The trainer spoke to the restless horse.

   He spoke firmly.

   He spoke calmly, too.

   The trainer spoke firmly to the restless horse, and he spoke calmly, too.

   _____

2. Miriam purchased an elegant gown.

   The gown was for her wedding.

   Miriam purchased an elegant gown, and it was for her wedding.

   _____

3. Our entire family sat on the couch.

   The couch was oversized.

   Our entire family sat on the oversized couch.

   _____

4. A singer entertained the crowd.

   She sang from ten until midnight.

   A singer entertained the crowd when she sang from ten until midnight.

   _____

   _____

5. Rocks poured out from the mouth of the volcano.

   The rocks were huge.

   They were fiery also.

   Huge, fiery rocks poured out from the mouth of the volcano.

   _____

Check Up

Read the underlined sentences. Choose the sentence below that correctly combines the underlined sentences.

1. The orchestra played Mozart selections.

   The orchestra played skillfully.

   A The orchestra played skillfully, and they played Mozart selections.

   B The orchestra skillfully played Mozart selections.

   C Playing in a skillful way, the orchestra played Mozart selections.

   D The skillful orchestra played Mozart selections.

2. Jorge bought a sweater at the shop.

   The sweater is brown.

   It is wool.

   F Jorge bought a sweater that is brown and wool at the shop.

   G Brown and wool is the sweater Jorge bought at the shop.

   H Jorge bought a brown wool sweater at the shop.

   J Jorge bought a sweater at the shop, and it is brown wool.

3. Books were stacked on the shelves.

   They were stacked neatly.

   A Books were stacked on the shelves in neat piles.

   B Books were stacked and stacked neatly on the shelves.

   C Books were on the shelves, and they were stacked neatly, too.

   D Books were neatly stacked on the shelves.

4. Ann chose bold stripes for the wallpaper.

   The paper is in her office.

   F In her office, Ann chose bold stripes for the wallpaper.

   G Ann chose bold stripes for the wallpaper, and it is in her office.

   H Ann chose bold stripes for the wallpaper in her office.

   J The wallpaper is in Ann's office and has bold stripes.

5. The mechanic changed a tire.

   He worked quickly.

   A The mechanic quickly changed a tire.

   B The mechanic worked quickly and also changed my tire.

   C The tire was changed by a quick mechanic.

   D Working quickly, the mechanic also changed a tire.

6. The basketball player dribbled the ball skillfully.

   She dribbled down the court.

   F Down the court skillfully the basketball player dribbled.

   G The basketball player dribbled the ball skillfully, and she dribbled down the court.

   H The basketball player dribbled the ball skillfully down the court.

   J Skillfully down the court, the basketball player dribbled.

Sentence Clarity: Misplaced Modifiers

Adding details to your writing usually makes it more interesting. However, adding a detail in the wrong place in a sentence may make your writing confusing. Consider this example:

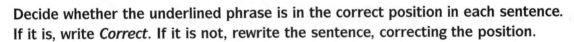

> My son picked blossoms for me hanging on the bush.

Was the speaker hanging on the bush? The poor placement of the underlined phrase suggests that meaning. The confusion is avoided by moving the modifying phrase:

> My son picked blossoms hanging on the bush for me.

A descriptive phrase that is placed in a sentence so that it describes the wrong person or thing is called a **misplaced modifier**. Avoid misplaced modifiers by placing every descriptive phrase as close as possible to the word it modifies.

Decide whether the underlined phrase is in the correct position in each sentence. If it is, write *Correct*. If it is not, rewrite the sentence, correcting the position.

1. Standing in the pond, you can see a heron.

   _____

2. The children brought mail addressed to me who live next door.

   _____

3. The piano in the corner of the room cannot be moved by anyone.

   _____

4. Janet joined the health club for more exercise in her office building.

   _____

5. All the vegetables lying on the lower shelf are from our garden in the refrigerator.

   _____

6. Printed in large letters, the newspaper headline can be seen from across the street.

   _____

Practice

When correcting sentences with misplaced modifiers, you sometimes discover that there is no word in the sentence for a modifier to describe. Consider this example:

Sitting in the waiting room, time passed slowly.

The sentence does not identify *who* is sitting in a waiting room. A phrase that is not connected to any word in its sentence is called a **dangling modifier**. To get rid of a **dangling modifier**, add the word described by the modifier. You will also have to change the wording slightly.

Sitting in the waiting room, *I found that* time passed slowly.

Compare each pair of sentences. Choose the sentence that is written correctly with no misplaced or dangling modifiers.

1. A   Driving through the thick fog, several accidents occurred.

    B   Driving through the thick fog, several drivers were in accidents.

2. A   Arriving late at the restaurant, Vince examined the menu.

    B   Vince examined the menu, arriving late at the restaurant.

3. A   With an excellent memory, this puzzle is easy.

    B   This puzzle is easy for anyone with an excellent memory.

4. A   Video games with tricky movements attract many players.

    B   Video games attract many players with tricky movements.

5. A   Elliot asked his teacher, confused by the test item, a question.

    B   Confused by the test item, Elliot asked his teacher a question.

6. A   Reading modern mysteries, Sherlock Holmes appears in many tales.

    B   Reading modern mysteries, I found that Sherlock Holmes appears in many tales.

7. A   Often police officers walking a beat stop criminals.

    B   Often police officers stop criminals walking a beat.

8. A   When boiling, mix the chopped apples in the syrup.

    B   When the syrup is boiling, mix the chopped apples in it.

Apply

Read the passage and look at the numbered, underlined parts. Choose the answer that is written correctly for each underlined part.

(1)   Yesterday I took my two nieces to the county zoo. Aged five and seven, I always enjoy taking the girls for short trips. I had the children wear colorful

(2) crowns on their heads to avoid losing them in the crowd. The children

(3) especially enjoyed Monkey Island. Climbing on the trees on the island, the girls were fascinated by the monkeys. We watched them for half an hour.

    Another group of animals that we will remember well is the lions.

(4) Watching the lions, our happy mood changed. At first everythng was fine.

(5) Then one lion frightened my nieces, roaring loudly. A visit to the Butterfly House calmed everyone down. At the end of the day, the girls agreed they had a great time.

1. **A** I always enjoy taking the girls, aged five and seven,

    B I, aged five and seven, always enjoy taking the girls

    C Always aged five and seven, I enjoy taking the girls

    D Correct as it is

2. **F** I had the children wear colorful crowns to avoid losing them in the crowd on their heads.

    G To avoid losing them, I had the children wear colorful crowns on their heads in the crowd.

    H To avoid losing them in the crowd, I had the children wear colorful crowns on their heads.

    J Correct as it is

3. **A** The girls, climbing on the trees on the island, were fascinated by the monkeys.

    B The girls were fascinated by the monkeys climbing on the trees on the island.

    C Climbing on the trees, the girls were fascinated by the monkeys on the island.

    D Correct as it is

4. **F** Watching our happy mood changed the lions.

    G Watching the lions, we lost our happy mood.

    H Our happy mood changed, watching the lions.

    J Correct as it is

5. **A** lion loudly frightened my nieces, roaring.

    B roaring lion frightened my nieces, loudly.

    C lion, roaring loudly, frightened my nieces.

    D Correct as it is

Check Up

Read each set of sentences. Choose the sentence that is written correctly. Make sure the sentence you choose has no misplaced or dangling modifiers.

1. A Everybody got wet because of the automatic sprinkler at the lawn party.

   B In my purse, I lost my keys.

   C Walking three abreast on the sidewalk, there's no room for anyone else.

   D Abner invented a game that became wildly popular.

2. F Television watchers followed the exciting series across the nation.

   G Most of the children attending this school live within walking distance.

   H After working in the office for a while, the job will become easier.

   J Customers can get a 10 percent discount on tickets if over 60 years old.

3. A Research by Dr. Bright's team revealed errors in earlier projects.

   B Swinging wildly, the ball was hit deep into left field.

   C At the amusement park, hundreds of people waited for a ride that turns its riders upside down in a long line.

   D That construction worker has a large family climbing the pole.

4. F Listening to *The 1812 Overture*, cannons fire at the end.

   G None of the keys opened the door that we carried.

   H Walking quickly, Anna easily arrived at the bus stop before the bus came.

   J Nelson ate a snack in his cab of raisins.

5. A The sign warns people not to cross the street when flashing.

   B A stray dog chased a skunk across my backyard that I had never seen before.

   C Each icon at the top of the screen has a different purpose.

   D Mr. Andrews received a bid from the contractor after a month of six thousand dollars.

6. F After mowing it three times, your new lawn should be fertilized.

   G Stretching from one end of the building to the other, the artist painted a seascape.

   H She cleaned the house for the visitors with enthusiasm.

   J People who work at the bankrupt company are worried about their jobs.

Sentence Clarity: Parallel Structure

The term **parallel structure** describes the use of balanced, or similar, elements in a sentence or passage. Usually these elements are compound sentence parts. Here are some examples of parallel structure:

Angela and Felix play oboes. (compound subject; both subjects are nouns)

The conductor selects the music, prepares the musicians, and leads the orchestra in a performance. (compound predicate; each predicate includes a verb and an object)

The orchestra played a symphony and a sonata. (compound object; both objects are nouns)

Tap the rhythm softly or watch the conductor's baton for the beat. (compound sentence; both clauses are independent, and both have the understood *you* as their subject)

The music is difficult to play but easy to enjoy. (compound adjective phrases; each modifying phrase includes an adjective and a verb phrase)

Read each pair of sentences. Choose the sentence with parallel structure.

1. **A** Four-year-old Jennifer likes ice cream and going to the movies.

   B Four-year-old Jennifer likes eating ice cream and going to the movies.

2. **A** The gardener weeded, trimmed, and watered the plants.

   B The gardener weeded, trimmed, and he was watering the plants.

3. **A** The way you dress and using the right words are important in a job interview.

   B The way you dress and how you speak are important in a job interview.

4. **A** Oliver's invention is inexpensive, useful, and nobody ever thought of it before.

   B Oliver's invention is inexpensive, useful, and unique.

5. **A** The black car that has a dented fender and drips oil is for sale.

   B The black car whose fender is dented and dripping oil is for sale.

6. **A** My neighbor's older son has no ambition but kind to animals.

   B My neighbor's older son has no ambition but is kind to animals.

Practice

Verbs have several forms. For a sentence to be parallel, two or more verbs must take the same form. Compare these examples:

Parallel Structure: The band <u>marched</u> and <u>played</u> music. (both verbs in past tense form)

Parallel Structure: The band <u>was marching</u> and <u>playing</u> music. (both verbs in present participle form, following the helping verb *was*)

Nonparallel Structure: The band <u>marched</u> and <u>was playing</u> music.

Read each sentence, giving special attention to the underlined verb or verb phrase. Choose the answer that completes the sentence and is parallel to the underlined sentence part.

1. Jesse was <u>hoping</u> and _____ of <u>attending</u> college.

   A dream

   B dreamed

   C dreaming

   D will dream

2. Jean <u>sang alto</u> and _____ for the school's choir.

   F wrote music

   G write music

   H writing music

   J will write music

3. The twins <u>ran onto the playground</u> and _____.

   A taking seats on the seesaw

   B took seats on the seesaw

   C to take seats on the seesaw

   D to be taking seats on the seesaw

4. At each of her annual reviews, Millie <u>has received excellent ratings</u> and _____.

   F was giving a bonus

   G gave a bonus

   H to give a bonus

   J has been given a bonus

5. The band <u>released a new album</u> and _____.

   A announce a U.S. tour

   B announces a U.S. tour

   C announced a U.S. tour

   D will announce a U.S. tour

6. The baby <u>smiles</u> and _____ every time her mother plays peek-a-boo with her.

   F will laugh

   G laughs

   H laughed

   J laughing

Apply

Read the paragraph and look at the numbered, underlined parts. Choose the answer that is written correctly for each underlined part. Make sure that sentences with compound parts have parallel structure.

      Most stores allow shoppers to pay with cash, to write a personal check,
(1) or some people use a charge card. The problem with using cash is that you
(2) might not have enough with you and, therefore, not buying what you want.
Some stores distrust personal checks. Showing several pieces of identification
(3) and to give extra information, such as your phone number, make using a
check time-consuming. Credit cards are easy to use—in fact, too easy! For many
(4) people, the monthly bill is more than they can pay and to create a problem.
(5) They must carry a balance, and they soon owe a great amount in interest charges.
(6) If you have a credit card, use it carefully and being sensible.

1. A using a charge card

   B you can use a charge card

   C to use a charge card

   D Correct as it is

2. F to not buy what you want

   G cannot buy what you want

   H are not buying what you want

   J Correct as it is

3. A when you have to give extra information,

   B giving extra information,

   C all the extra information you have to give,

   D Correct as it is

4. F creating a problem

   G creates a problem

   H to cause or create a problem

   J Correct as it is

5. A soon owing a great amount in interest charges

   B they soon owed a great amount in interest charges

   C soon a great amount owed in interest charges

   D Correct as it is

6. F sensibly

   G showing sense

   H with good sense

   J Correct as it is

Check Up

Read each sentence and look at its underlined part. Choose the answer that is written correctly for the underlined part.

1. Either the plant has a disease or it simply needs fertilizer.

   A needing fertilizer

   B sometimes you simply have to feed plants

   C if it simply needs fertilizer

   D Correct as it is

2. Traffic can be snarled by construction, when there's an accident, or by gawkers.

   F by an accident

   G if an accident happens

   H because of an accident

   J Correct as it is

3. To develop responsibility, children watch younger siblings, help in the kitchen, and to keep their own bedrooms clean.

   A keeping their own bedrooms clean

   B keep their own bedrooms clean

   C kept their own bedrooms clean

   D Correct as it is

4. Fans of Hollywood movies expect beautiful scenery and for the actors to sing and dance in beautiful costumes.

   F to see lavish musical numbers

   G enjoying lavish musical numbers

   H lavish musical numbers

   J Correct as it is

5. Please get to the bus stop on time and to save an empty seat for me.

   A saving an empty seat

   B saved an empty seat

   C save an empty seat

   D Correct as it is

6. We ought to find the car's owner and telling him or her about the flat tire.

   F that we'll tell him or her

   G tell him or her

   H that he or she should know

   J Correct as it is

7. Neither the blue paper on the shelf nor the pink paper in the storeroom is right for this job.

   A getting the pink paper from the storeroom

   B where the pink paper is

   C to use the pink paper in the storeroom

   D Correct as it is

8. Jeff was identifying what must be done and organized the people who would do it.

   F organize

   G organizing

   H will organize

   J Correct as it is

Review

Complete Sentences, Fragments, and Run-Ons

Every complete sentence has a subject and a predicate. The subject names who or what is doing something. The predicate contains the verb and tells what the subject is doing.

Every guest at the party | has brought a food dish.

    subject   predicate (verb is underlined)

A **fragment** lacks at least one of these parts. Correct a fragment by providing the missing part or parts.

A **run-on sentence** runs together two or more sentences with no punctuation or only a comma between the sentences. Correct a run-on sentence by punctuating and capitalizing correctly.

Sentence Combining: Compound Parts and Modifiers

To avoid repetitive short sentences, combine sentences by forming **compound parts.**

Eliza brought tuna salad. Jeff brought tuna salad.

Eliza and Jeff brought tuna salad.

To avoid a series of short sentences on a single topic, combine the sentences by moving modifiers.

Guests were hungry. They ate all the food. They ate quickly.

Hungry guests quickly ate all the food.

Sentence Clarity: Modifiers and Structure

A modifier placed so that it describes the wrong word is called a **misplaced modifier.** Move a misplaced modifier to the correct place.

With a note from his mom, the teacher admitted the late boy.

The teacher admitted the late boy with a note from his mom.

If there is no word in the sentence for a modifier to describe, it is a **dangling modifier.** Revise the sentence by giving the modifier something to describe.

Dangling modifier: Without a car, it's hard to get to work.

Correct: Without a car, I find it hard to get to work.

Use the same type of word in each of the compound parts in a sentence. Mixing various types produces **nonparallel structure.**

Nonparallel: To be or not being, that is the question.

Parallel: To be or not to be, that is the question.

Assessment

Read each set of sentences. Then choose the sentence that is written correctly. Be sure the sentence you choose is complete, that its modifiers are placed correctly, and that it uses parallel structure.

1. **A** Because the tree was dying.

    B Before cutting the heavy branch, the worker tied a rope around it.

    C The rope went through a pulley, it was fastened to the tree trunk.

    D Another worker helped by holding the end of the rope and to guide the cut branch down.

2. **F** The British and we use the same words we say many differently.

    G The word *laboratory*, for instance.

    H On the second syllable, the British place the emphasis.

    J It has been said we are separated by a common language.

3. **A** To be successful, a magazine ad must get a reader's attention.

    B It must be bright it must be clever.

    C We remember ads that make us think or giving us a laugh.

    D Competitions for the best of the ads in various categories.

4. **F** Gave him three yellow tomatoes, almost golden.

    G How much fertilizer is needed for growing vegetables?

    H I enjoy growing vegetables and to cook things from my garden.

    J Grow tomatoes in new areas each year they use up the soil.

Read the paragraph and look at the numbered, underlined parts. Choose the answer that is written correctly for each underlined part.

(5) Both the leaders of the Romans and the Romans using language contributed
(6) to the names of months. For example, Julius Caesar and Augustus Caesar gave their names to July and August, who were Roman emperors. September got its name from the Latin word for *seven*, because it was originally the seventh month of the year.

5. **A** and when the Romans used language

    B and the language of the Romans

    C and the Romans to use language

    D Correct as it is

6. **F** Augustus Caesar gave their names, who were Roman emperors, to July and August

    G Augustus Caesar gave their names to July and August. Were Roman emperors

    H Augustus Caesar, who were Roman emperors, gave their names to July and August

    J Correct as it is

Assessment continued

Read each set of underlined sentences. Choose the sentence below that correctly combines the underlined sentences.

7. Candace plays tennis well.

   She plays golf well also.

   She bowls poorly.

   A Candace plays tennis and she plays golf well but bowls poorly.

   B When Candace plays tennis or golf, she does well, but she bowls poorly.

   C Candace plays tennis well and golf well, but bowling she does poorly.

   D Candace plays tennis and golf well but bowls poorly.

8. Students are raising money for the class trip.

   They are raising money by selling candy bars.

   F Students raising money for the class trip, and the way that they're doing it is by selling candy bars.

   G The candy bars that the students are selling are for the class trip.

   H The students who are selling candy bars are doing it to raise money for the class trip.

   J Students are raising money for the class trip by selling candy bars.

9. The mall on Euclid Avenue has an Italian restaurant.

   The mall on Main Street has an Italian restaruant.

   A The mall on Euclid Avenue has an Italian restaurant, but the mall on Main Street does, too.

   B The mall on Euclid Avenue and on Main Street has an Italian restaurant.

   C The malls on Euclid Avenue and Main Street have Italian restaurants.

   D There are Italian restaurants at many malls, including the one on Euclid Avenue and the one on Main Street.

10. The garden at Weston Park has gravel walks.

    The garden at Weston Park has brick walks.

    F The garden at Weston Park has gravel and brick walks.

    G There are gravel walks and brick walks in the garden at Weston Park.

    H The garden at Weston Park has gravel walks, and it has brick walks.

    J The garden with gravel walks and brick walks is at Weston Park.

11. Benjamin asked his friends for advice.

    Benjamin asked his family for advice.

    He wanted advice about health insurance.

    A Benjamin asked his friends and family for advice, and the advice was about health insurance.

    B When Benjamin wanted advice about health insurance, he asked his friends and family.

    C Benjamin asked his friends and family for advice about health insurance.

    D Benjamin asked his friends for advice about health insurance, and his family.

12. Adelaide moved to a townhouse.

    She moved from her large apartment.

    She moved recently.

    F Adelaide moved to a townhouse, but until recently she had been living in a large apartment.

    G Adelaide recently moved from her large apartment to a townhouse.

    H Adelaide moved from her large apartment recently, and she moved to a townhouse.

    J When Adelaide moved from her large apartment recently, she moved to a townhouse.

13. The smoke alarm needs new batteries.

    The flashlight needs new batteries.

    A Not only the smoke alarm needs new batteries, but also the flashlight does.

    B The smoke alarm needs new batteries, and the flashlight needs new batteries.

    C Whenever the smoke alarm needs new batteries, so does the flashlight.

    D The smoke alarm and flashlight need new batteries.

The Main Idea of a Paragraph

A writer groups several sentences together to create a paragraph. These sentences work together to form a complete thought called the **main idea**. Often one sentence states the main idea of the paragraph. It is called the **topic sentence.**

The first sentence in the following paragraph is a topic sentence. It tells readers that the paragraph will be about simple ways to prepare a home for a power failure. You will notice that the writer has not included details about anything other than this topic.

<u>It is not hard to prepare your home for a power failure</u>. Keep a few flashlights handy. Make sure that they have fresh batteries. Keep a supply of candles and matches in case the power is out for a while. Use a battery-operated alarm clock, or make sure that your plug-in clock has a battery back-up.

The topic sentence is general enough to allow for several examples. It is also narrow enough to limit what the writer can describe—just preparations for a power failure.

Circle the letter beside the main idea of each paragraph. Underline its topic sentence.

1.   Charles got great news from the palm reader. She said that he would enjoy good health for a very long time. She predicted that his marriage might go through a rocky period. However, it would remain strong. She revealed that if he took risks in his career, they would surely pay off. She even saw great wealth in his future.

   A Palm readers are always correct in their predictions.

   B The palm reader gave Charles great news.

   C The palm reader said that Charles would be rich someday.

2.   Pickled foods can be found in all parts of the world. Korea is famous for kim chee, which is pickled cabbage. Chinese cooking uses pickled eggs and ginger. In Mexico you can find pickled jalapeños. In the American South you'll see pickled beans, okra, and onions. And inside your hamburger bun, of course, lies a pickled cucumber.

   F Korean cooks make kim chee, which is pickled cabbage.

   G You can find pickled foods in all parts of the world.

   H All foods around the world are pickled.

Practice

Read each paragraph below. Choose its topic sentence from among the five lettered sentences. Write the letter of the topic sentence on the blank line.

A For the U.S. soldiers in the Old West, bad food was the real enemy.

B Liza and laundry just don't mix.

C When you travel with your baby, you'll be packing many things into your car.

D The covered wagons that pioneers used were crowded, to say the least.

E Penelope is a devoted soap opera fan.

1. _____. She works nights so that she is able to see the soaps during the day. When she can't be home, she sets her VCR to record them. She subscribes to several soap opera magazines. She and her friends have long discussions about what the characters are doing. She even named her pets after soap opera stars!

2. _____. Their diet was made up almost solely of salted meat, beans, potatoes, and coffee. They hardly ever had fruits or vegetables. Rations arrived at the forts rotten and moldy. More soldiers died due to poor diet than were killed in frontier battle.

3. _____. Her T-shirts and sweat socks are all pink because she washes them with her red shirts. One time she used so much soap that suds poured out all over the floor. Last week she got something stuck in the lint trap, and the dryer caught fire. We put the fire out, but who knows what will happen next!

4. _____. Wagons were only four feet wide and ten feet long. A wagon had to be packed with everything that the family owned. Many treasured items were left behind to make room for food, medicines, and weapons. The jam-packed wagons had to serve as the family's home for four to five long months.

5. _____. Even to go on an overnight visit, a baby needs quite a few items. Of course, he or she will need diapers and two or more changes of clothes. Mealtime needs include favorite foods along with special dishes, spoons, and bottles or cups. Don't forget to throw in some blankets and a baby seat. If you're lucky, there will still be room enough for you and the baby, too!

Apply

Write a topic sentence for each of the following paragraphs. (The topic sentence in these paragraphs is the first sentence.)

1. _____. Last month, the museum's courtyard was full of huge stone sculptures. Indoors there was a gorgeous exhibit of paintings from India. Right now there is a show of famous abstract paintings in one hall. The plans for next month include a display with wild laser beams dancing across the walls and ceiling.

   _____

   _____

2. _____. They can be made from a variety of fruits for a variety of tastes. They have a nice texture that can be made either chunky or smooth. They can range from very mild to hot and spicy. Chutneys can be used as sauces, sides, spreads, or even as pizza toppings.

   _____

   _____

3. _____. Tools should be stored where you can reach them quickly and easily. Many people hang them from hooks on the wall. Different sized nails and screws should be kept in different containers. That way you won't grab the wrong size by mistake. Ropes, extension cords, and cords of power tools should be wound up after use. That way they won't get tangled or knotted.

   _____

   _____

4. _____. The Spanish missionaries felt at home in California's warm, dry climate. It was like that of their homeland. They found that plants from Spain did well in their new home. They decided that the California coast was perfect for establishing towns. In fact, the priests and brothers were so enthusiastic that they built 21 missions there.

   _____

   _____

Check Up

Read each paragraph. Then choose the best topic sentence for each paragraph.

1. _____. The seated statue of Lincoln gazes out over the Reflecting Pool. Inscribed on the walls are two of the famous speeches Lincoln gave. One mural shows the Angel of Truth freeing a slave. Another mural shows the unity of the North and the South.

   A Lincoln was a great president.

   B Lincoln was shot at the theater.

   C The Lincoln Memorial is in Washington, D.C.

   D There is much to see at the Lincoln Memorial.

2. _____. In 1396 the queen of Denmark declared that an inn be built every 20 miles along the country's main roads. In 1500 the law was changed to provide an inn every ten miles. The tradition of kindness continues today. Modern travelers can find a good bed and a meal wherever they go in Denmark.

   F Danish inns are better than hotels.

   G For centuries, Denmark has been a good place to travel.

   H Denmark's history is interesting.

   J In Denmark, if you close your inn you could be arrested.

3. _____. It makes him happy when his students learn. He likes leading discussions about insects, rainbows, and other science topics. Most of all, he enjoys experiments.

   A There are over 700,000 known species of insects.

   B Allen knows a lot about insects.

   C Allen is an excellent scientist.

   D Allen loves being a science teacher.

4. _____. There is a large grocery store right across the street from her apartment. Right on the corner is her favorite Italian bakery. The library is two blocks away. Best of all, Donna works right next door to where she lives.

   F Donna's home is on the bus line.

   G Donna found a job that she likes.

   H Donna has everything she needs right in her neighborhood.

   J Donna enjoys Italian foods.

5. _____. Its red color always made it stand out from other planets and the stars. Mars became even more interesting when scientists discovered strange markings on it. People wondered if the markings were really canals dug by Martians.

   A People have always been fascinated by the planet Mars.

   B Martians may invade Earth.

   C Mars is becoming a vacation spot.

   D The atmosphere on Mars would be deadly to humans.

Finding the Topic Sentence

Many paragraphs include a topic sentence, which states the main idea. Often the topic sentence comes at the beginning of the paragraph. It directs readers and lets them know what they can expect from the paragraph.

It is not easy to become a taxi driver in London. To become licensed, cabbies have to pass a difficult exam. They must memorize all the basic driving routes. They must be able to locate every major building and tourist attraction. On average, a London cabbie trains for three years before getting a license.

The topic sentence does not always come at the beginning of the paragraph.

The city of Cuernavaca is located about an hour south of Mexico City. Those who live in Cuernavaca can easily travel to the capital for work or for weekend fun. The city itself has much to offer. It has beautiful architecture and a thriving nightlife. It is filled with flowers and trees. Its nickname is "The City of Eternal Spring." All in all Cuernavaca is a great place to live.

Details about life in Cuernavaca are presented throughout this paragraph. At the end of the paragraph, the author summarizes the details in a topic sentence.

Underline the topic sentence in each of the following paragraphs.

1.   The ancient Greeks believed that different gods controlled different parts of the weather. The sun god was Helios. The winds were controlled by the god Aeolus. Zeus was the ruler of the heavens. He controlled the clouds, rain, and thunder.

2.   At the pageant, Miss Georgia had flowers woven into her braids. Miss Michigan had hair extensions all the way down to her knees. Miss Pennsylvania had cornrows with rubies at the ends. Miss Nevada had her hair in a towering red beehive. All of the contestants had imaginative hairstyles.

3.   Good habits can help you study better. Pick a study spot with as few distractions as possible. Don't tempt yourself by studying in front of the TV. Set up all necessary items before you begin to study. If you don't have to keep getting up for pencils, notebooks, coffee, or other items, you can concentrate better. Give yourself a reward after a good study session.

Practice

Read each paragraph. Then choose its topic sentence.

1.   The Tour de France is a long and challenging bicycle race. The race takes place every summer over a three-week period. Some parts of the course are flat. Other parts go through mountains, requiring a great deal of strength and endurance. Usually the hot July sun adds stress on the teams of cyclists. By the time the competitors have completed the course from Luxembourg to Paris, they have cycled 2,036 miles!

   A By the time the competitors have completed the course from Luxembourg to Paris, they have cycled 2,036 miles!

   B The race takes place every summer over a three-week period.

   C The Tour de France is a long and challenging bicycle race.

2.   The Ford Motor Company has one car called the Mustang and another called the Bronco. Mercury has the Cougar. Dodge makes a truck and a van called the Ram. And, of course, there is a whole line of cars called Jaguars. Naming cars after powerful animals seems to be a popular practice.

   F The Ford Motor Company has one car called the Mustang and another called the Bronco.

   G Naming cars after powerful animals seems to be a popular practice.

   H Dodge makes a truck and a van called the Ram.

3.   The English countryside is known for its churches. In the town of Norwich alone there are 32 churches from the medieval period. The church at the abbey in Bath is a favorite of visitors. The Wells Cathedral, which is 800 years old, is believed to be the most beautiful church in Great Britain.

   A The church at the abbey in Bath is a favorite of visitors.

   B In the town of Norwich alone there are 32 churches from the medieval period.

   C The English countryside is known for its churches.

4.   Jim and Jack were twins separated at birth. They were reunited at the age of 35 and discovered some strange similarities. Both Jim and Jack married women named Linda. Both had two sons. Both drove blue cars. They both liked woodworking and vacationed in Florida. Often twins are amazingly alike.

   F Often twins are amazingly alike.

   G Jim and Jack were twins separated at birth.

   H Both Jim and Jack married women named Linda.

Apply

The topic sentence is missing in each of the following paragraphs. On the lines below each paragraph, write a topic sentence for the paragraph.

1. _____. You can learn to speak Spanish, Italian, or Chinese with other adults. You can study music or history. Why not try a class in painting or photography taught by local artists? For those who want something more active, there are classes in tango and tap dancing.

   _____

   _____

2. One kind of monkey, the pygmy marmoset, is only about six inches long. The douroucouli monkey, when fully grown, measures about 19 inches. The woolly monkey can grow to a length of 23 inches. The mandrill, one of the largest monkeys, can reach a length of 32 inches. _____.

   _____

   _____

3. _____. Citizens of Portland, Oregon, jog and bicycle every day of the year. They also ski year-round on nearby Mount Hood. Western Oregon's rivers and coasts offer these folks all kinds of water sports. The area is so sports-minded that two major sports equipment companies have their headquarters there.

   _____

   _____

4. _____. The clothes in Jake's closet are all neatly pressed and arranged. His bed is always made with military corners. His medicine cabinet is organized alphabetically. If you run your finger over any surface in his house, you'll never find a speck of dust.

   _____

   _____

Check Up

Read each paragraph. Then choose its topic sentence.

1. _____. If you dream that you lose your wallet, it may be time to examine your sense of identity. If you lose your car in a dream, you might want to look at your need for independence. If you dream that you lose your keys, you may really be afraid of losing authority.

   A We dream so that we are not bored while we sleep.

   B Most people don't always remember their dreams.

   C Dreams of lost objects may be trying to tell you something.

   D For the last few nights, my dreams have been very strange.

2. _____. One legend says that a goatherd named Kaldi noticed that his goats sometimes acted frisky. Later, he realized that the friskiness happened after the goats had nibbled at a certain shrub. He tasted some berries from the shrub himself. He felt filled with energy. That may be how humans began enjoying caffeine!

   F Legend has it that goats are smarter than other animals.

   G Legends can help us to understand animals such as goats.

   H According to legend, you have goats to thank for your morning coffee.

   J Goatherds always have milk in their coffee.

3. _____. For example, you may be so absorbed in a book that you miss your subway stop. Or you may be watching TV so closely that you feel like you're part of the action. Mild hypnosis even includes times when you're working so hard you don't realize how much time has passed.

   A Hypnosis is an effective way to change your habits.

   B You may experience mild forms of hypnosis in your daily life.

   C Mild hypnosis is better than deep hypnosis.

   D Once, the Amazing Millwort hypnotized a whole stadium full of people.

4. Have you ever heard Los Angeles called "City of Angels"? This nickname comes directly from translating its Spanish name into English. _____. "Tinseltown" alludes to the movie-star flashiness of the city. "Surf City" comes from the many surfers who use the city's beaches. A less kind nickname, "Hell Town," comes from the old Wild West days, when L.A. was known for being lawless.

   F Los Angeles has many nicknames.

   G Los Angeles boasts pleasant temperatures year-round.

   H Most people who live in Los Angeles have nicknames.

   J Los Angeles should be called "Fancyland."

Developing Paragraphs with Details and Examples

Each sentence in a paragraph should contribute to its overall idea or picture. Sometimes a topic sentence introduces the idea or outlines the picture. The rest of the sentences are **supporting sentences.** They give more information or complete the picture.

In descriptive paragraphs, supporting sentences often give **sensory details.** These details tell how something looks, sounds, smells, feels, or tastes. Reading these details, the reader can almost feel as if he or she is experiencing the thing described.

> Ana was enchanted by the midnight luau in Hawaii. A bonfire crackled and sent sparks into the dark sky. The night air was salty and cool all around her. The sand was soft and wet between her toes. She sipped a drink from a tart, sweet pineapple. She could hear the steady ocean waves beneath the music and the laughter.

In other paragraphs, supporting sentences give **examples.**

> There are several simple ways to deal with chronic back pain. Why not try drinking more water to lubricate your joints? Another home remedy is taking vitamins to aid your body in repairing itself. Regular exercise has also proven to be helpful.

Underline the topic sentence of each of the following paragraphs. Then decide whether the paragraph is developed using examples or sensory details. Write *Examples* or *Sensory Details* on the line.

1.   Dublin, Ireland, was home to many famous writers. Jonathan Swift, who wrote *Gulliver's Travels*, lived in Dublin. The author of *Dracula*, Bram Stoker, was also a Dubliner. Writers Oscar Wilde, James Joyce, and George Bernard Shaw were all raised in Dublin.

   _____

2.   Visiting my grandmother's house is like going back in time. Heavy curtains cover all of the windows. The rooms are dark and musty. Smells of rosemary and lavender hang in the air. Scratchy music plays on an old Victrola. We drink tea with milk and sugar and nibble on ginger cookies.

   _____

Practice

Read each of the following paragraphs. Decide how each is developed. Circle either *examples* or *sensory details*. Then read the sentences below the paragraph. Choose the sentence that best supports and develops the main idea of the paragraph.

1.   Asthma attacks can be triggered in many ways. _____. Tobacco smoke, car exhaust, and other pollutants often have the same effect. Even foods like cheese, nuts, and dried fruits can set off a bout of asthma.

This paragraph is developed using (examples, sensory details).

A Dust, pollen, and other airborne substances can bring on attacks.

B My brother has had asthma since he was a toddler.

C The word *asthma* comes from the Greek language.

2.   On a perfect May day in the park, Jolene's father proposed to her mother. _____. The sun was bright and warm on their faces. Robins and bluebirds chirped in the trees overhead. Sitting on a bench with a heart carved into it, Jolene's father popped the question.

This paragraph is developed using (examples, sensory details).

F Many people get engaged in the spring.

G The rich perfume of lilacs filled the air.

H Frank's father proposed to his mother in December.

3.   A variety of careers is available for people who like to travel. _____. Magazines and newspapers are often looking for travel-related articles. Working as a travel agent is another possibility. Agents help others plan their trips, and they sometimes get discounts on their own travel. Finally, becoming a flight attendant for an airline is a sure way to get places. Bon voyage!

This paragraph is developed using (examples, sensory details).

A Traveling alone can be fun if you play it safe.

B The community college is hosting a career fair this weekend.

C Travel writing is one option.

Apply

Read each paragraph. On the lines provided, write one more supporting sentence that would fit in the blank. Follow the directions in parentheses.

1.   A trip to the circus is a sensation all its own. Jangling music surrounds you as you take your seat. The tastes of buttery popcorn and sweet cotton candy mix on your tongue. Colorful clowns and acrobats cartwheel by in a rush. _____. (Add a sentence with a sensory detail.)

_____

_____

2.   There are many ways to entertain yourself on a long car ride. You can count cars of a certain color or model. You can make up words from the letters on license plates. You can play alphabet or trivia games. _____. (Add a sentence with an example.)

_____

_____

3.   Yesterday I gardened in the rain. The soil was soft, dark, and moist beneath my feet. I could hear the hush of raindrops on the leaves. The herbs and flowers smelled fresh. _____. (Add a sentence with a sensory detail.)

_____

_____

4.   The summer gives us a wide assortment of fruits. Strawberries arrive early in summer. Later we get raspberries, blackberries, and blueberries. Watermelon is a summer fruit, and so is cantaloupe. _____. (Add a sentence with an example.)

_____

_____

5.   When the holidays come, I have a chance to eat some of my favorite foods. I allow myself to enjoy buttery cookies and pastries. I don't hold back when the juicy ham is set in front of me. _____. (Add a sentence with an example.)

_____

_____

Developing Paragraphs with Details and Examples **115**

Check Up

Read each topic sentence. Then choose the answer that best develops the topic sentence.

1. The neighbors made me miserable with their all-night party.

   A They moved here last August from Alaska. They are always commenting on how hot it is here.

   B I like parties where people dress in costume. It adds an element of mystery to the night.

   C I try to be a good neighbor. I am always willing to loan my neighbors my tools or lend a hand when needed.

   D The pulsing beat of their music wouldn't let up. They burned meat on their grill, and the smoke poured in through my window.

2. In the Corbières region of France, the simple life lives on.

   F Some residents raise bees and make their own honey. Some have small goat farms and make cheese.

   G Corbières is about five hours from Paris. It is close to the border with Spain.

   H People in France consume much more wine than Americans do. Wine is served with most French meals.

   J The writer Henry Thoreau encouraged people to live simply. He himself lived a simple life for a time in a small cabin.

3. When Buckingham Palace was first built, nothing in it worked.

   A Queen Victoria was in power when Buckingham Palace was completed. The period of her reign is called the Victorian era.

   B Besides being the London residence of the Queen, Buckingham Palace is a busy headquarters. It is also the site of important royal ceremonies.

   C The doors would not close properly. The drains did not function, and the bathrooms smelled.

   D A small part of Buckingham Palace is now open to visitors. Some British citizens are angry because they cannot visit the entire palace.

Developing Paragraphs with Reasons, Facts, and Figures

Paragraphs can be developed in a variety of ways. Often a topic sentence states the main idea. The other sentences expand upon, explain, or support the main idea. Sometimes, a paragraph's sentences present **reasons** to support its main idea.

> I think that Lillian should move to New York City. As an artist, she'd have access to many museums, galleries, and opportunities. Lillian likes a fast-paced environment, and New York can offer her one. She enjoys meeting new people, and there are eight million of them in New York.

The topic sentence suggests that Lillian should move to New York. The other sentences provide reasons to back up the idea.

In other paragraphs, **facts and figures** develop or support the main idea.

> Termites construct tall mounds above their nests. African termite mounds often reach a towering height of 25 feet. That feat is similar to humans making a skyscraper six miles high!

Decide whether the underlined sentence in each paragraph is the topic sentence or a supporting sentence. Write *Topic Sentence* or *Supporting Sentence* on the line.

1. <u>Tea plants thrive under the right conditions</u>. Tropical climates with average temperatures of over 80 degrees are good for most teas. Locations where the rainfall is 80 to 100 inches a year work especially well. The finest teas are grown at elevations of 3,000 to 6,000 feet, where they mature more slowly.

   _____

2. The movie I saw last night was a real winner. The plot took unexpected twists and turns. <u>The acting was wonderful</u>. The special effects were very well done. Most important, the strong female characters sent a powerful message to young women.

   _____

Practice

Read each paragraph. Decide whether the supporting sentences develop the paragraph with reasons or with facts and figures. Write *Reasons* or *Facts and Figures* on the line.

1.   The Murphy Building on West Main Street is one of the finest examples of Civil War architecture in town. Famous leaders and writers have dined in its first-floor restaurant. The current occupants of the upper floors are volunteers for human rights, and they can't afford to move elsewhere. Clearly, the unique Murphy Building should not be torn down.

_____

2.   Jupiter is by far the largest planet in our solar system. It has 2.5 times more mass than all of the other planets put together. Its mass is 318 times greater than that of Earth. Jupiter is made up mostly of gas but has a rock core which is itself twice the size of our planet.

_____

3.   In 2001 baseball player Barry Bonds broke the record for most home runs in a season. He hit 73 home runs that year. Of those home runs, 37 were hit at his home stadium in San Francisco. A total of 17 were hit off left-handed pitchers, while 56 were hit off right-handed pitchers. The longest home run that Bonds hit traveled a whopping 480 feet. Bonds was deservedly named Most Valuable Player of the National League for 2001.

_____

4.   After careful thought, Louise decided to turn down Henri's proposal of marriage. He wants to live in France, but she doesn't want to leave her family in the United States. He doesn't seem to like children, and Louise plans to have at least three. He likes to stay out all night, and she is a morning person.

_____

5.   We need to hire another night clerk at the store. There are sometimes too many customers for one clerk to handle efficiently. Besides, it isn't really safe to have an employee working all by herself so late. And it doesn't make sense that the clerk should have to lock up the store every time she takes a break.

_____

Apply

Read each paragraph below. Decide how it is developed. Circle either *reasons* or *facts and figures*. Then choose the sentence that best works in the paragraph to support and develop the main idea.

1.   It is a good idea for children to have pet dogs. From the time they are puppies into their old age, dogs make excellent companions for children. Taking care of a dog teaches important lessons in responsibility. Walking the dog can provide regular exercise. _____.

This paragraph is developed using (reasons, facts and figures).

   A   The most popular household pets must surely be dogs and cats.

   B   Finally, every child can benefit from the love that a dog gives its owner.

   C   Dogs can sometimes bring annoying fleas into their owners' homes.

2.   Dinosaurs came in a wide range of sizes. The largest known dinosaur was found in New Mexico. It measured about 120 feet from head to tail and was about 18 feet high. The smallest known dinosaur was found in Portugal. _____.

This paragraph is developed using (reasons, facts and figures).

   F   This tiny dinosaur was only about three feet long.

   G   No one knows how or why dinosaurs disappeared from the earth.

   H   Many dinosaurs ate only plants and may have been gentle animals.

3.   Paul and Vivienne just bought a huge old house in the country. It sits on four acres of land. The house is 2,400 square feet, nearly twice the size of their present house. The living room is 18 by 20 feet. _____.

This paragraph is developed using (reasons, facts and figures).

   A   Vivienne just got a raise at work, so she wants to redecorate.

   B   The couple is looking forward to the quiet peace of country life.

   C   The gracious dining room measures about 15 by 16 feet.

4.   Alex prefers working the afternoon shift to the morning shift. He likes to spend time with his grandmother in the mornings. _____. He even prefers the afternoon manager to the morning manager.

This paragraph is developed using (reasons, facts and figures).

   F   Alex is 24 years old and hopes to be a manager someday.

   G   He also likes to go to the gym before work.

   H   To get this job, Alex answered a blind ad in the newspaper.

Check Up

Read each topic sentence. Then choose the answer that best develops the topic sentence.

1. Samuel always studies a company before he buys its product.

   A He has a twin brother who works at the same company. People constantly mix them up in the hallways.

   B He buys a cup of coffee and a newspaper every morning. On the way home he buys candy for his daughter.

   C He wanted to be a detective when he was younger. He changed his mind and became a travel agent.

   D He doesn't want to support companies whose employees work in unsafe conditions. He believes in the power of informed consumers.

2. It will be a miracle if Sharese passes her chemistry exam.

   F She is taking chemistry, French, and math. She likes math the best.

   G Her chemistry teacher claims that he discovered a new element.

   H Instead of studying last night, she went out dancing. She arrived ten minutes late for the exam and didn't hear the instructions.

   J She is the best dancer in New York. They know her at all of the clubs.

3. The British Cheese Awards selected a new champion last year.

   A There were 596 different cheeses entered in the competition. Britain's finest cheese experts, chefs, and food writers served as judges.

   B Brie is a soft cheese made in France. It is easy to spread on crackers.

   C The British comedy group Monty Python did a famous skit about a cheese shop. The shop didn't have any cheeses the customer wanted.

   D Some people say that the best cheeses are aged for a year or more. Cheese can be aged underground or in cool, dark rooms.

4. A blizzard is an uncommonly dangerous type of winter storm.

   F Blizzards carry strong winds and freezing temperatures. They have been known to drop five feet of snow or more.

   G My brother Neville was born during a blizzard. He is now a sled racer.

   H Winter brings shorter days and longer nights. The cold air and snow often keep people indoors.

   J You should watch where you step, in case there is an icy patch. An average of 21 injuries occur in Ohio every year due to slipping on ice.

Recognizing the Order of Events

Writers often present events in a story or steps in a process in time order. Sometimes the writer uses key words such as *first, second, next, then, after that, finally,* and *last* to show the order of events.

> Victor opens the tuxedo shop in the mall every morning at 9:00. First, he unlocks the gate and raises it high enough to duck inside. Second, he turns on the lights. Next, he inventories the tuxedos to be picked up that day. After that, he takes money out of the safe and puts it into the cash register. Finally, he raises the gate all the way and turns on the OPEN sign.

In the following paragraph, the order of events is clear even without the use of key words.

> Anne-Marie painted her bedroom last Saturday. She began by moving as much furniture as she could out of the room. The rest she covered with plastic. Before she started to paint, she put masking tape around the windows and the door. She painted all day. When she was done, she took off the tape and plastic and moved the furniture back.

Read the following paragraph. Then choose the correct answer to each question.

> Charlotte and Pete won a free trip to Manhattan, and they tried to see it all in one day. They had an early breakfast uptown and took a stroll in Central Park. Before noon, they visited The Metropolitan Museum of Art. They bought hot dogs from a street vendor for a quick lunch. They spent most of the afternoon shopping. They had a big dinner and then listened to some jazz in Greenwich Village. Before going back to their hotel, they went dancing. By the end of the night, they were exhausted.

1. What did Charlotte and Pete do just before visiting the museum?

    A They bought hot dogs from a street vendor.

    B They spent most of the afternoon shopping.

    C They took a stroll in Central Park.

2. What did they do after listening to jazz in Greenwich Village?

    F They visited the Museum of Natural History.

    G They went dancing.

    H They had a big dinner.

Practice

Read each topic sentence and the four sentences below it. Number the sentences in time order from 1 to 4.

1. Ben Franklin used simple means to prove that lightning was electric.

   _____ When a storm came, he attached a key to a kite, using a long wire.

   _____ He sent the kite up into the air.

   _____ He waited for a thunderstorm to hit.

   _____ Lightning hit the kite, went down the wire, and electrified the key.

2. Before modern ovens came to Finland, there was a daily order to cooking.

   _____ The large stone oven was fired up as soon as the family awakened.

   _____ Meat stews and pots of rice were put in the oven at night, to cook slowly while the oven cooled down.

   _____ In the morning, while the oven was hottest, potato pastries were made.

   _____ As the oven cooled a little, breads and cookies were baked.

3. Today was the first day of the trial.

   _____ The witness left the stand in tears, and the judge called a recess.

   _____ The prosecutor and the defense attorney both questioned the witness about her relationship with the defendant.

   _____ After the statements, the first witness was called.

   _____ It began with opening statements by the prosecution and defense.

4. Lorraine spent the afternoon painting in the meadow.

   _____ She painted lots of green grass and leaves on the canvas.

   _____ When it started to get dark, she packed up for the day.

   _____ She set up her easel and squeezed paint onto her palette.

   _____ With her palette knife, she mixed blue and yellow to make green.

5. It took the writer three years to complete his historical novel.

   _____ Then he read over the draft and carefully revised it.

   _____ When he had enough information, he spent a year writing the draft.

   _____ He began by doing intensive research at the library.

   _____ Finally, he worked with his editor on the finishing touches.

Apply

Read the topic sentence of each paragraph. Then read the four sentences below it. These sentences are out of order. Fill the blank spaces of the paragraph with the letters of the correct sentences.

1.   The python has an elaborate way of killing its prey. First, _____.
Next, _____. Then, _____. Last, _____.

   A it squeezes the trapped prey hard enough to kill it.

   B it bites the unsuspecting prey with its many sharp teeth.

   C while the prey is stunned by the bite, the python coils its long body around the prey.

   D the python unhinges its jaw and swallows the prey whole.

2.   Pistachios are harvested in the Greek islands in late August. First, _____.
Next, _____. Then, _____. Finally, _____.

   F canvas sheets are spread beneath trees.

   G the soaked nuts are left to dry on rooftops in the sun.

   H the tree branches are shaken so that the nuts fall onto the canvas.

   J the nuts are hulled and soaked in seawater.

3.   The wedding supper was lovely. First, _____. Next, _____.
Then, _____. Last, _____.

   A the dinner plates were cleared, and the best man gave a toast.

   B the guests milled around cheerily before finding their assigned seats.

   C the bride and groom, still laughing from the toast, went to cut the wedding cake.

   D servers brought soup, salad, and roasted chicken to the seated guests.

4.   Shortening a pair of pants is easy. First, _____. Next, _____.
After that, _____. Last, _____.

   F fold the inch under, and crease it with an iron.

   G measure how long you want the legs to be.

   H sew the folded, creased cuff in place and put the pants on!

   J cut off the extra material, leaving an inch longer than your measurement.

Check Up

In each paragraph, details are presented in time order. However, one sentence is missing. Read each paragraph. Then choose the sentence that belongs in the blank.

1.   Serious tea lovers brew their tea a certain way every time. They begin by filling the kettle with cold water and bringing it to a rolling boil. Next, they pour some of the boiling water into the teapot, swirl it around, and pour it out again. This is called "warming the pot." _____. After that, they pour the boiling water over the leaves and let it sit for three to five minutes. Finally, they are ready to sit back and enjoy.

A Then they nibble on cookies while they drink their tea.

B Then they measure one spoonful of tea leaves per cup and place the leaves in the pot.

C Then they add milk and sugar to the tea.

D Then they light the burner on the stove.

2.   The Vipers Little League team came from behind to win in the last inning. They started the inning behind the Huskies, 5–2. The first batter hit a double and ran to second base. _____. The third and fourth batters struck out. The fifth batter hit a single, which loaded the bases. The sixth batter was little Jimmy Gorman. He swung on the first pitch and hit a home run over the fence.

F With the bases loaded, the coach came out to talk to the pitcher.

G Next week, the Vipers will play the Cougars.

H The second batter drew a walk, so there were two Vipers on base.

J The second batter was Mark D'Angelo.

3.   The bank robbers put on their clown masks. They walked into the bank and yelled for everybody to get down onto the floor. They handed a large sack to the teller. _____. They ran with their loot out to their getaway car and sped down the block.

A The police headed them off at the intersection.

B She didn't know what to do with it.

C They took off their clown masks and threw them in the dumpster.

D She filled the sack with money and gave it back.

Identifying an Unrelated Sentence

Every sentence in a paragraph has a function. The topic sentence, if the paragraph has one, states the main idea. The other sentences support or give details about that idea. If a sentence does not relate to the main idea, it does not belong in the paragraph.

In the following paragraph, the first sentence states the main idea—how Janine made a good impression. The other sentences should give details about that idea. However, the underlined sentence, while it touches on a related subject, does not develop the main idea. It should be removed.

Janine made a good impression in her job interview. She wore a tasteful gray business suit and sensible shoes. Her handshake was firm and confident. Some people's handshakes are too soft. Her answers, questions, and comments were clear and to the point.

Read the following paragraph. Then choose the correct answer to each question.

Tim and Sarah have named all their children after rock stars. Jimi, the oldest, is named after Jimi Hendrix. He was all-state wrestling champion last year. The twins are named Sonny and Cher. The little girl is named Madonna, though everyone calls her Maddie for short. Just last month they welcomed baby Elvis into the family.

1. What is the main idea of this paragraph?

   A Children should not be named after celebrities.

   B The baby's name is Elvis.

   C One family's children are named after rock stars.

   D Sonny and Cher were rock stars.

2. Which sentence does not tell more about the main idea?

   F Jimi, the oldest, is named after Jimi Hendrix.

   G He was all-state wrestling champion last year.

   H The twins are named Sonny and Cher.

   J Just last month they welcomed baby Elvis into the family.

Practice

Read each paragraph. Cross out the sentence in the paragraph that does not belong. Then answer the two questions that follow.

1.   One of America's favorite breakfasts is pancakes. Maple syrup is made from the sap of the sugar maple tree. In spring, the sugary sap flows from the tree's roots and trunk to its branches. Farmers tap into the tree and collect the sap. Then they boil it down to make maple syrup.

What is the main idea of this paragraph? _____

Why should the crossed-out sentence be removed?

_____

2.   September has always been Holly's favorite month. Holly enjoys the excitement of the opening of the school year. She loves the changing colors of the leaves and the start of football season. Holly roots for the Pleasanton Pheasants. Finally, Holly likes September because she was born September 19.

What is the main idea of this paragraph? _____

Why should the crossed-out sentence be removed?

_____

3.   Melisa gets most of her clothing at secondhand stores. Her favorite dress was first worn during the years when Dwight Eisenhower was president. He had been a World War II general. She has a pair of platform shoes that were popular during the 1970s. The beaded bag that completes the outfit comes from the 1920s.

What is the main idea of this paragraph? _____

Why should the crossed-out sentence be removed?

_____

4.   Some people believe that baseball is a dying sport in America. They say that Americans prefer the fast action of football and basketball. As further evidence of baseball's loss of appeal, they point out that young people are playing less baseball and more soccer. In Europe, soccer is called football.

What is the main idea of this paragraph? _____

Why should the crossed-out sentence be removed?

_____

Apply

Read each of the following paragraphs. If all the sentences are related to the main idea, write *Correct* on the line. If one sentence is unrelated, cross it out.

1.   The Black Death was a disease that killed millions of people in Europe and Asia during the fourteenth century. It was spread by rat fleas. First the fleas made the rats sick. After the rats died, the fleas jumped to nearby humans. Within hours, a person could die. Many city dwellers see rats in their neighborhoods even today.

_____

2.   Nothing can keep Mariah down. Although her parents did not value education, Mariah was a top student. When they refused to help her with her college bills, she got two jobs to pay her way through school. State colleges are usually cheaper than private ones. Even though it took her six years, she finally graduated from college.

_____

3.   A volcanic eruption can be a deadly natural force. In A.D. 79, a volcano erupted in Italy and destroyed the city of Pompeii. In 1902 an eruption killed about 30,000 in Martinique. An 1815 eruption in Indonesia killed 92,000 people. You can see an active volcano in Hawaii.

_____

4.   Driving a race car takes great concentration. When you are moving at 150 miles per hour, accidents can happen quickly. You are making turns every few seconds, so you can't let your mind wander even for a moment. Other drivers may pull into your path, so you must always know where they are and how fast they are going.

_____

5.   American cities are getting bigger all the time. City limits are creeping outward. People are moving to new, outer suburbs and abandoning old city centers. Philadelphia is a historic city in Pennsylvania. This expansion is called urban sprawl.

_____

Check Up

Read each paragraph. Then choose the sentence that does not belong.

1.   **1.** Nicole volunteers at the community hunger center once a month. **2.** There she fills shopping bags with non-perishable food items. **3.** Value Market has some of the best deals on canned goods. **4.** She hands out the bags to needy people who take them home to feed their families.

    A Sentence 1

    B Sentence 2

    C Sentence 3

    D Sentence 4

2.   **1.** The Amish live in the modern world but are not part of it. **2.** They are not allowed to use electricity. **3.** They may not watch television. **4.** They travel using horses and buggies. **5.** Some Amish men are excellent carpenters.

    F Sentence 1

    G Sentence 3

    H Sentence 4

    J Sentence 5

3.   **1.** Nadia has a strange ability. **2.** If you give her almost any date, she can tell you what day of the week it falls on. **3.** The Western world uses the Gregorian calendar. **4.** She can repeat this feat for any date from 1950 to 2050.

    A Sentence 1

    B Sentence 2

    C Sentence 3

    D Sentence 4

4.   **1.** Many people suffer from unexplained, senseless fears called phobias. **2.** The *ph* in phobia sounds like *f*. **3.** People with claustrophobia can't stand enclosed spaces. **4.** People who fear spiders suffer from arachnophobia.

    F Sentence 1

    G Sentence 2

    H Sentence 3

    J Sentence 4

Transition and Connective Words

A writer must make sure readers understand clearly the relationship between ideas in a paragraph. It's not enough to present events, details, or reasons one after another. Transition words are needed to connect one sentence to the next.

In the following paragraph, transitional words that connect the sentences are underlined.

> Joe had never voted in an election. However, he was not happy with the current leader's policies. Therefore, he wanted to vote the man out of office. First, he registered to vote. Then he went to the polls and cast his ballot. Finally, he celebrated when his candidate won.

Listed below are common transition words and the connections and relationships they make clear.

Time: after, as soon as, at first, before, finally, immediately, last, meanwhile, next, often, when

Place: around, below, beside, in front of, inside, opposite, outside, over, there, within

Cause and Effect: as a result, because, consequently, for that reason, so, therefore

Compare or Contrast: besides, even so, however, in spite of, nevertheless, on the other hand, similarly

Example: for example, for instance

Order of Importance: first, more important, primarily

Conclusion: finally, in conclusion, in summary

Underline the transition word or phrase in each item below. Then circle the relationship that the transition makes clear.

1. Karen hates cold weather. So she moved to Arizona.
   example   time   cause and effect

2. Catch the bird. Immediately band its leg and let it go.
   contrast   time   conclusion

3. Woodpeckers eat insects in dead trees. Similarly, sapsuckers feed off trees.
   place   order of importance   compare

Practice

Each paragraph below is missing one sentence. Read the five lettered sentences at the top of the page. For each paragraph, choose the sentence that makes the best transition. Write the letter of that sentence on the line.

A In contrast, we're now seeing temperatures shoot up faster than ever before.

B Finally, animals can't move to other climates because the animals are crowded out by humans.

C For those reasons, there is more carbon dioxide in the air now than ever before.

D Because of global warming, the planet is changing.

E Consequently, the ground has sunk more than fifteen feet.

1.   Did you know that the icecaps at the North and South Poles are melting? _____. A temperature increase of one or two degrees may seem minor, but it's enough to cause widespread problems.

2.   Temperatures have shifted before. For example, a thousand years ago Europe had mild winters. Wine grapes even grew in England. Then what scientists call the little ice age drove temperatures down. Rivers froze and the amount of snow increased. But those changes happened gradually. _____.

3.   For centuries we've been burning coal, oil, and gas, which pour carbon dioxide into the air. We've cleared the trees that would have soaked up heat-trapping gases. _____.

4.   First, scientists noticed that glaciers are melting. In parts of Alaska, the permafrost has thawed. _____.

5.   The change in climate is already affecting plants and animals. As winter temperatures have increased, the number of penguins in the Antarctic has fallen. Some butterflies are near extinction because hotter, drier weather has killed the plants they feed on. _____.

Apply

Read each paragraph. Then choose the transition that works best to complete the paragraph.

Anyone can learn to build a bookcase. **(1)** _____ , find some plans in a woodworking magazine or on the Internet. Then buy quality, unwarped boards. Oak is very solid and good for furniture. **(2)** _____ , pine works too and is cheaper. The store will often cut them to the lengths you need. Sand the boards and put them together with wood screws. **(3)** _____ , stain and varnish your new bookcase.

Therefore   However   Finally   First

Jane goes for a walk every day after dinner. It reduces stress from her job and gives her more energy. Because she wants to breathe better and walk faster, walking also has helped her quit smoking. **(4)** _____ , her husband watches TV after dinner, cigarette in hand.

On the other hand   Finally

Origami is the art of folding paper into sculptures. A computer scientist taught himself to fold curved shapes and repeating 3-D units like chains of cubes. From the outside, one model looks like just a rolled-up sheet of paper. **(5)** _____ , however, it's a miniature spiral staircase.

Consequently   Inside

Kevin enjoys gardening. He especially likes spring bulbs. **(6)** _____ , he planted red tulips and white crocuses in the front yard. He planted sweet-smelling hyacinths in a window box. **(7)** _____ , he planted daffodils all along a path out back.

Meanwhile   For example   Finally

In August 2003, a huge power failure blacked out most of the Northeast and Midwest. **(8)** _____ , researchers collected air samples while flying over central Pennsylvania. They found a 90 percent drop in sulfur dioxide in the air. **(9)** _____ the blackout, visibility increased by more than 2.5 miles.

Because of   The next day   Finally

Check Up

Read each paragraph. Then choose the letter of the sentence with the transition that best fills in the blank.

1. Some wild animals adapt very well to living near humans. Deer, for example, are thriving in the suburbs. What homeowners see as landscaping, the deer see as an all-you-can-eat buffet. They don't care how expensive the plants are. _____.

   A Finally the weather gets cold, and deer come into yards and eat evergreens right next to houses.

   B In spite of when the weather gets cold, deer come into yards and eat evergreens right next to houses.

   C Outside, the weather gets cold, and deer come into yards and eat evergreens right next to houses.

   D As soon as the weather gets cold, deer come into yards and eat evergreens right next to houses.

2. Shauna is training for the Olympics. Her sport is gymnastics. She specializes in the uneven bars. _____. A gymnast has to have very strong arms to lift her body in the air and maneuver it around the bars. It's time consuming to work out with weights, but that's what it takes to be the best.

   F Besides, she does weight training too.

   G Consequently, she does weight training too.

   H Meanwhile, she does weight training too.

   J Similarly, she does weight training too.

3. Animals have been learning human language. An African grey parrot has a vocabulary of over two hundred words. A chimpanzee knows American Sign Language. A dog named Rico has a big vocabulary and is still learning new words. _____. Rico realizes that the name he never heard before refers to the new toy.

   A When a new toy is added to Rico's toy box, his owner asks for it by name.

   B Before a new toy is added to Rico's toy box, his owner asks for it by name.

   C For example, if a new toy is added to Rico's toy box, his owner asks for it by name.

   D Because a new toy is added to Rico's toy box, his owner asks for it by name.

Main Idea and Topic Sentence

Writers group their sentences in paragraphs. All the sentences in a paragraph should work together to tell about one idea, called the **main idea.** Often, the main idea is stated in a **topic sentence.** A topic sentence that begins a paragraph introduces the main idea to readers. A topic sentence at the middle or end of a paragraph usually summarizes or restates the main idea.

Developing Paragraphs with Supporting Sentences

Sentences that tell more about the main idea are called **supporting sentences.** In some paragraphs, writers use supporting sentences to describe **sensory details** about how a person or thing looks, sounds, smells, tastes, or feels. In other paragraphs, they use supporting sentences that give **examples**, **facts and figures**, or **reasons** to develop the main idea.

Sequence

When writing about events or describing step-by-step processes, it often makes sense to present details in **time order.** Sometimes, the writer uses key words such as *first, second, next, then, after that, finally,* and *last* to make the order of events clear to readers.

Unrelated Sentences

Every paragraph has a main idea, whether it is stated in a topic sentence or not. All the sentences in a paragraph should relate to the main idea. Writers have a responsibility to write and then edit their work carefully, removing any sentence that does not directly develop the paragraph's main idea.

Transition and Connective Words

Every sentence in a paragraph must relate not only to the main idea but also to the sentences that come before and after it. To write clear paragraphs, writers make connections between ideas. Transition words like *meanwhile, often, therefore, however,* and *finally* connect ideas and sentences.

Assessment

Read each paragraph. Choose the sentence that best fills the blank.

1. _____. First, the builders cut blocks of hard snow about three feet by one and one-half feet. Then they place the blocks in a big circle. Layer by layer, they position the blocks closer together until, at last, they meet in a dome in the middle. Two holes are cut: one on the side, for the door, and another in the roof, to serve as a vent. Finally, the igloo is ready to be lived in.

   A Inuit people rarely construct igloos anymore.

   B It would be uncomfortable to live in an igloo.

   C Constructing an igloo is a painstaking process.

   D Snow blocks have excellent insulating qualities.

2. _____. During the first stage, your brain is still quite active from your day. You may focus on one idea after the other in quick succession. In the second phase, you experience light sleep. The third stage is a quiet sleep, which prepares you for the fourth stage, a deep sleep. These stages are repeated and reversed throughout the night.

   F Sleep is important for your health.

   G Without sleep, people cannot concentrate during the day.

   H Most people need eight hours of sleep every night.

   J A typical sleep cycle has four stages.

3. Trish recorded minutes at the committee meeting. _____. Then she proofread what she had typed. She printed one copy of the report and then ran off twenty copies, one for each committee member. Last, she placed a copy in each committee member's mailbox.

   A Next, she stood in line to use the copying machine.

   B Afterwards, she typed up a draft of the minutes on her computer.

   C Then she e-mailed a copy to the committee chairperson.

   D She brought her notebook and a pen into the meeting room.

4. Autumn is my favorite season. The air smells crisp and fresh. The sky is bright blue and the leaves are turning vivid colors. It feels like a new start. _____

   F As a result, it also means snow, ice, and bitter cold are coming soon.

   G Besides, it also means snow, ice, and bitter cold are coming soon.

   H On the other hand, it also means snow, ice, and bitter cold are coming soon.

   J More important, it also means snow, ice, and bitter cold are coming soon.

Assessment continued

Read each topic sentence. Then choose the answer that best develops the topic sentence.

5. People around the world build their homes using materials that are easily available.

   A Architects study for years to learn how to design public buildings and private homes. Usually an architect works with a contractor to build a home.

   B Some of the materials used in the homes of the wealthy are quite expensive. The more expensive and rare a material is, the more it proves the owner's social position.

   C Homes built near the San Andreas Fault must be strong enough to withstand an earthquake. No one knows when the predicted big earthquake will happen.

   D The Navajo people built their homes, called hogans, using logs and earth from the land around them. The Inuit used snow blocks from their home in the frozen Arctic to build temporary homes called igloos.

6. All winter, Kris relived her hike up the mountain on that summer morning.

   F The Rocky Mountains are a young mountain range. The Appalachian Mountains, on the other hand, are quite old.

   G Again, she felt the cool breeze against her skin. She heard the sweet songs of the birds. She saw the green mountain against the blue sky.

   H She is planning next year's vacation now. She hopes to visit Hawaii or Alaska.

   J It is always a wise idea to hike with a companion. If you have an accident, it's comforting to know that someone is there to help you.

7. Many Americans experienced terrible problems during the Great Depression.

   A The Depression began in 1929. That was the year of the stock market crash.

   B At the beginning of the Great Depression, Herbert Hoover was president. Franklin Roosevelt became president in 1932.

   C Some families lost all their money and their homes. Without any income, they were forced to stand in long lines just to get something to eat.

   D People who lived through the Depression are careful with money. They know how easily it can disappear.

Assessment continued

Read each of the following paragraphs. Then choose the sentence that does not belong in the paragraph.

8.   **1.** The early Olympic Games lasted only five days. **2.** On the first day, a huge parade was held. **3.** Jim Thorpe of the United States won gold medals in the 1912 Olympics. **4.** Competitions were held on the second, third, and fourth days. **5.** A dinner to honor the winners took place on the fifth day.

    F Sentence 1

    G Sentence 2

    H Sentence 3

    J Sentence 4

9.   **1.** Niagara Falls has attracted daredevils for decades. **2.** A man called Blondin walked a tightrope above the Falls several times. **3.** Many people have gone over the Falls in barrels. **4.** Niagara Falls is beautiful at any time of the year.

    A Sentence 1

    B Sentence 2

    C Sentence 3

    D Sentence 4

10.   **1.** Jean is determined to become a good cook. **2.** Jean has always been just a few pounds overweight. **3.** She subscribes to a magazine that is filled with cooking tips and techniques. **4.** She has enrolled in a well-known cooking school.

    F Sentence 1

    G Sentence 2

    H Sentence 3

    J Sentence 4

11.   **1.** In 1815, a volcano erupted in Asia. **2.** Volcanic ash flew seventeen miles into the air. **3.** The ashes blocked out sunlight as far away as the United States. **4.** Mount Saint Helens is a famous volcano. **5.** Because the ashes in the air kept temperatures low, Americans called 1815 the "year without a summer."

    A Sentence 2

    B Sentence 3

    C Sentence 4

    D Sentence 5

Capitalizing Proper Nouns and *I*

Proper nouns name particular persons, places, or things. When you write, always capitalize proper nouns.

Capitalize the names of people. Capitalize every word and initial in a person's name.

> Shirley Temple Black   John F. Kennedy

Often, titles such as *Doctor* and *Mayor* are used before names. **Titles and their short forms, or abbreviations, should be capitalized when they appear before names.**

> The name of our neighbor is Dr. Dailey.
>
> Have you met Mayor Harris? She is our new mayor.

Capitalize words for family relations when they are used with or in place of the names of particular people. When these family titles follow possessive pronouns such as *my, our,* or *your,* do not capitalize them.

> I sent notes to Aunt Sara but not to my other aunts.
>
> I called Mom. Did you call your mother?

Always capitalize the pronoun *I*.

Underline the words in each sentence that should be capitalized.

1. Do you know that cousin michael plays drums in a band?

2. The last time i saw uncle charles was several years ago.

3. My sister worked with both judge kim and senator blake.

4. The writer mary ann evans used the pen name george eliot.

5. Address your envelope to mrs. linda j. helm.

6. My friend, governor mike a. thompson, served two terms.

7. Tell aunt carla she has an appointment with dr. saunders.

8. My grandfather, coach davis, and i had dinner together.

9. The speaker was superintendent barbara dade.

10. My meeting with prof. lewis was brief.

Practice

Read each pair of sentences. Circle the letter of the sentence with correct capitalization.

1. **A** My new Manager is carlos estevez.

   B My new manager is Carlos Estevez.

2. **A** The picture shows mr. Bryant S. Lane speaking to the Governors.

   B The picture shows Mr. Bryant S. Lane speaking to the governors.

3. **A** Last year I worked with Uncle Roger.

   B Last year i worked with uncle Roger.

4. **A** Here is the present Abby bought for her Grandmother.

   B Here is the present Abby bought for her grandmother.

5. **A** In this picture, Princess Carol is being held by her father.

   B In this picture, princess Carol is being held by her Father.

Read each of the following items. Capitalize words wherever necessary. Write *Correct* if the item is written properly.

6. our grandmother _____

7. senator jennifer spencer _____

8. Timothy a. Hamilton _____

9. uncle Fred _____

10. professor Butler _____

11. mr. eugene h. clark _____

12. one congressman _____

13. dr. steven j. garofalo _____

14. alex t. dixon _____

15. w.c. fields _____

Apply

Rewrite each of the following sentences with correct capitalization.

1. We hired mr. jeff reynolds to take pictures at the wedding.

   _____

2. The street was named for general robert e. lee.

   _____

3. My grandfather and uncle louis love to go fishing.

   _____

4. Your tour guide will be ms. diana carr.

   _____

5. My father and i met mr. blair in dr. chin's office.

   _____

6. We are having a dinner in honor of coach lopez.

   _____

7. Have you seen the old photos taken by grandpa brady?

   _____

8. She and erica have applied for the job of security guard.

   _____

9. Both mayor g.w. lang and councilman bill weld were reelected.

   _____

10. My friends and i listened to some old records by jimi hendrix.

    _____

Check Up

Read each set of sentences. Choose the sentence that has correct capitalization.

1. **A** The winner of the marathon was Jesse d. Franklin.

   B We hired t.s. Edwards last week.

   C The Quarterback on the team is Jon K. Stuart.

   D This form needs the signature of Aaron S. Marks.

2. **F** When do you expect mr. Owens to arrive?

   G Our new Secretary is Ms. Michell.

   H These flowers are for Mrs. Wendell.

   J The office of dr. Blake is on the seventh floor.

3. **A** The house Aunt Bonnie bought is only six years old.

   B I was told that uncle George was a Police Officer for many years.

   C The truck I drive used to belong to my Cousin.

   D Yesterday I visited my Grandmother.

4. **F** This parking spot belongs to Principal Carlson.

   G The Surgeon will be Doctor Susan Yee.

   H The bill was submitted by senator Barbara Littell.

   J The Judge answered the Lawyers' questions.

Read each sentence and look at the underlined words. Choose the answer that is written correctly for the underlined words.

5. We always take our pets to dr. frazer.

   A dr. Frazer

   B Dr. Frazer

   C Dr. frazer

   D Correct as it is

6. Our house was built by J.P. Lemanski.

   F j.p. lemanski

   G J.P. lemanski

   H j.p. Lemanski

   J Correct as it is

7. I hope aunt Jenny can come to the reunion.

   A Aunt jenny

   B aunt jenny

   C Aunt Jenny

   D Correct as it is

8. The company's founder was mr. L. Escobaar.

   F mr. l. Escobar

   G Mr. L. Escobar

   H Mr. l. Escobar

   J Correct as it is

Capitalizing Proper Nouns and Proper Adjectives

Capitalize names of days, holidays, and months. Do not capitalize the names of the seasons.

> Monday   Halloween   September   winter

Capitalize the names of cities, states, and countries.

> Atlanta   Georgia   Germany

Capitalize the names of streets, buildings, and bridges.

> Skyline Drive   Hancock Tower   Brooklyn Bridge

Capitalize the names of clubs, organizations, and businesses.

> Bay Garden Club   Boy Scouts   General Motors

Capitalize geographical names. Capitalize words such as *north, east,* and *west* when they refer to a section of the country. Do not capitalize words that refer to a direction.

> The pioneers crossed the Rocky Mountains in the West.

> The Snake River is in the southern part of the state.

If a proper noun has more than one word, capitalize all important words. Do not capitalize *the, of,* or *in.*

> the Great Wall of China

Capitalize proper adjectives.

> Swiss army knife   Russian caviar

Underline the words in each sentence that should be capitalized.

1. Visit the field museum of natural history in chicago.

2. We ate belgian waffles and canadian bacon for breakfast.

3. My spanish class meets on wednesday.

4. The aleutian islands are southwest of alaska.

5. The springtown library is on bluebell street.

6. There is a big parade in new york city on thanksgiving.

7. The blair building is north of first street.

8. My son is a member of the claremont juggling club.

9. We are flying to paris, france, on american airlines.

Practice

Read each of the following items. Capitalize words wherever necessary. Write *Correct* if the item is written properly.

1. memorial day   _____

2. seattle, washington   _____

3. the month of may   _____

4. chrysler building   _____

5. national geographic society   _____

6. Lake erie   _____

7. southern new mexico   _____

8. mountains and plains   _____

9. rodeo drive   _____

10. on the avenue   _____

Read each of the following pairs of sentences. Choose the sentence with correct capitalization.

11. A The plainville ecology club offers trips in the Spring.

    B The Plainville Ecology Club offers trips in the spring.

12. A We visited the national Museum Of American History.

    B We visited the National Museum of American History.

13. A The Month of february has twenty-nine days this year.

    B The month of February has twenty-nine days this year.

14. A Go west for two streets and then turn north on Taylor Road.

    B Go West for two Streets and then turn North on Taylor Road.

15. A I heard that the Extreme Sportswear Company has opened a store in the Fuller Building.

    B I heard that the Extreme Sportswear company has opened a store in the Fuller building.

Apply

Rewrite each of the following sentences with correct capitalization.

1. We saw mount rushmore in south dakota last summer.

2. I bought a chair at jordan's furniture store.

3. We drove across the peace bridge over the niagara river.

4. This store sells bikes made by the prentiss company.

5. Have you seen the chinese paintings at the cleveland museum of art?

6. The french ship sailed through the panama canal.

7. Meet me at the corner of market street and powell street.

8. The city of houston, texas, is about fifty miles from the gulf of mexico.

9. I start working at mervyn's department store on saturday.

10. The mojave desert is in southern california.

Check Up

Read each set of sentences below. Choose the sentence that has correct capitalization.

1. **A** The Museum has an egyptian mummy.

   B Here in the North, we have very cold winters.

   C I am going to a concert on Friday, june 7.

   D The traffic is heavy on the callahan bridge.

2. **F** A ferry took the tourists to the Statue Of Liberty.

   G Head West on Concord Road.

   H Join the King Chess Club!

   J That was a great game at Yankee stadium.

3. **A** My grandfather was born in Milan, Italy.

   B We planted flowers on Earth day.

   C Open an account at first national Bank.

   D Cameras are on sale all Month!

4. **F** My aunt is a buyer for the Department Store.

   G Cactus grows in the Southwest.

   H We ski every Winter at Northstar Resort.

   J My uncle retired from the White motor company.

Read each sentence and look at the underlined words. Choose the answer that is written correctly for the underlined words.

5. Many businesses are moving into Western Nevada.

   A western nevada

   B western Nevada

   C Western nevada

   D Correct as it is

6. Crocodiles thrive in the swamps of Everglades national park.

   F everglades national park

   G everglades National Park

   H Everglades National Park

   J Correct as it is

7. Many people do not have to work on president's day.

   A President's Day

   B President's day

   C president's Day

   D Correct as it is

8. Our holiday fireworks display will take place on Thursday, July 3.

   F Thursday, july 3

   G thursday, July 3

   H thursday, july 3

   J Correct as it is

Capitalizing First Words and Titles

Begin every sentence with a capital letter.

    This vase is beautiful.   How much does it cost?

Capitalize the first word of every quotation.

    "Can I have the recipe for this dessert?" asked Bonnie.

    Mariah answered, "It is a family secret."

Capitalize the first word, the last word, and any other important words in a title. Do not capitalize *the, in, for, from, a, an, on, with, and, at,* or *by* unless it comes first or last.

    The Wizard of Oz (book and movie)

    The Daily Local (newspaper)

    "Song of Myself" (poem)

Capitalize many abbreviations. Abbreviations are shortened forms of words or phrases.

    Address your letter to P.O. Box 138.

    There are flights at 9:00 A.M. and 2:00 P.M.

Underline the words in each sentence that should be capitalized.

1. the restaurant opens at 6:00 a.m.

2. everyone cheered when the band played "the stars and stripes forever."

3. one of my favorite old movies is *the maltese falcon.*

4. the traveler complained, "these lines at the airport are too long."

5. one of the country's best newspapers is *the new york times.*

6. send your comments to p.o. box 8451.

7. "when can you start working?" asked the interviewer.

8. my friends thought *nightmare on elm street* was a scary movie.

9. the secretary asked, "do you have an appointment?"

10. *the twilight zone* was a great television series.

Practice

Read each of the following items. Capitalize words wherever necessary. Write *Correct* if the item is written properly.

1. *the sound of music* (movie) _____

2. *life on the mississippi* (book) _____

3. "the king of cotton candy" (poem) _____

4. *the wall street journal* (newspaper) _____

5. *candid camera* (television program) _____

6. "Casey at the Bat" (poem) _____

7. "the open boat" (short story) _____

8. *The New Yorker* (magazine) _____

Read each of the following pairs of sentences. Choose the sentence with correct capitalization.

9. **A** The bank teller asked, "would you like to open an account?"

   B The bank teller asked, "Would you like to open an account?"

10. **A** My dinner reservation is for 7:30 P.M.

    B My dinner reservation is for 7:30 p.m.

11. **A** "We may get up to a foot of snow," said the newscaster.

    B "we may get up to a foot of snow," said the newscaster.

12. **A** my friend asked, "Have you found a new job?"

    B My friend asked, "Have you found a new job?"

13. **A** The company's address is p.o. box 213.

    B The company's address is P.O. Box 213.

14. **A** the flight attendant reminded us, "buckle your seat belts."

    B The flight attendant reminded us, "Buckle your seat belts."

15. **A** Have you seen the movie *Cheaper by the Dozen*?

    B Have you seen the Movie *Cheaper By The Dozen*?

Apply

Rewrite each of the following sentences with correct capitalization.

1. "enjoy your meal," said the waiter.

   _____

2. this recipe is from *family circle*.

   _____

3. my alarm clock rings at 6:45 a.m.

   _____

4. did you read the article in *the washington post*?

   _____

5. mail your request to p.o. box 10.

   _____

6. "our first game will be tomorrow," said the coach.

   _____

7. the clerk asked, "can I help you?"

   _____

8. my sister's favorite book is *the old man and the sea*.

   _____

9. the salesman assured me, "this is a great car."

   _____

10. the poem "elegy for jane" is quite sad.

    _____

Check Up

Read each set of sentences. Choose the sentence that has correct capitalization.

1. **A** "Welcome to the museum," said the guide.

   B "tilt your head a bit," suggested the photographer.

   C the director boomed, "Speak loudly and clearly."

   D My neighbor asked, "may I borrow your lawn mower?"

2. **F** The story "The Cask Of Amontillado" has a grim ending.

   G we saw the ad in the *Ukiah daily journal.*

   H We get some useful repair tips from watching *Your old house and you.*

   J *A Day at the Races* is a silly but likable movie.

3. **A** The game begins, rain or shine, at 2:00 p.m.

   B can you meet us at the ticket office at 7:00 A.M.?

   C Address your letter to p.o. Box 415.

   D We finally got home at 11:00 P.M.

4. **F** "where does it hurt?" asked the doctor.

   G The plumber said, "The job will be finished in an hour."

   H My brother asked, "can you give me a ride to the airport?"

   J "we are out of that item," said the salesclerk.

Read each sentence and look at the underlined words. Choose the answer that is written correctly for the underlined words.

5. *Pride And Prejudice* is both a book and a movie.

   A *Pride and Prejudice*

   B *Pride and prejudice*

   C *pride and Prejudice*

   D Correct as it is

6. The gardener said, "these plants need a lot of water."

   F the gardener said, "These

   G The gardener said, "These

   H the gardener said, "these

   J Correct as it is

7. Mail your package to p.o. box 1256.

   A P.O. box 1256

   B p.o. Box 1256

   C P.O. Box 1256

   D Correct as it is

8. The secretary said, "Fill out these forms."

   F the secretary said, "Fill

   G The secretary said, "fill

   H the secretary said, "fill

   J Correct as it is

Review

Proper Nouns, Proper Adjectives, and *I*

Capitalize the names of people. Capitalize titles and their abbreviations.

      Barbara Jordan   General Patton   Dr. Stewart

Capitalize words for family relations when they are used with or in place of the names of specific people.

      Uncle Frank   Grandma Hayes   Mom

Capitalize the names of days, holidays, and months.

      Monday   Arbor Day   April

Capitalize the names of cities, states, and countries.

      San Jose   Montana   Italy

Capitalize the names of streets, buildings, and bridges.

      Richmond Road   Eiffel Tower   Franklin Bridge

Capitalize geographical names. Capitalize words such as *north*, *south*, and *west* when they refer to a section of the country.

      Missouri River   Mount McKinley   in the Northeast

Capitalize proper adjectives.

      Parisian café   Egyptian pyramid   Chinese food

Capitalize the names of clubs, organizations, and business firms.

      Camp Fire Girls   Xerox Corporation

Capitalize the pronoun *I*.

First Words and Titles

Begin every sentence with a capital letter.

      Do you need a ride?   We have room in our car.

Capitalize the first word of every direct quotation.

      "Who called?" asked Ed.   Jo replied, "It was your mother."

Capitalize the first, last, and any other important words in a title.

      Men in Black (movie)   *Tri-Valley Herald* (newspaper)

Capitalize many abbreviations such as P.O., A.M., and P.M.

Assessment

Read the following paragraphs and look at the numbered, underlined parts. Choose the answer that is written correctly for each underlined part.

(1)   The first meeting of the green thumb Garden Club will be
(2)   held on Friday, May 15. Our speaker will give a talk on famous
(3)   european gardens. We hope you can attend!

1. A Green Thumb garden club

    B Green Thumb Garden Club

    C Green thumb garden club

    D Correct as it is

2. F Friday, may 15

    G friday, May 15

    H friday, may 15

    J Correct as it is

3. A European Gardens

    B european Gardens

    C European gardens

    D Correct as it is

(4)   An accident took place in front of the engle Public Library this
(5)   morning. The first police officer on the scene was Sergeant Riley.
(6)   He stated, "unfortunately, the accident occurred during rush hour.
        Fortunately, nobody was injured."

4. F Engle Public Library

    G Engle public library

    H engle public Library

    J Correct as it is

5. A Sergeant riley

    B sergeant riley

    C sergeant Riley

    D Correct as it is

6. F Stated, "unfortunately

    G stated, "Unfortunately

    H Stated, "Unfortunately

    J Correct as it is

(7)   The planners of the annual fourth of july fireworks promise that
(8)   this year's show will be better than ever. If you want a seat, be sure
(9)   to arrive well before the starting time of 9:30 p.m.

7. A Fourth Of July

   B Fourth of July

   C fourth of July

   D Correct as it is

8. F this Year's

   G This Year's

   H This year's

   J Correct as it is

9. A 9:30 P.m.

   B 9:30 p.M.

   C 9:30 P.M.

   D Correct as it is

(10)   My Sister and I love to travel. It is exciting to go to places we have
(11)   never been and try things we have never done. For example, last Summer
(12)   we went white-water rafting on the colorado river. It was scary but fun!

10. F sister and i

   G Sister and i

   H sister and I

   J Correct as it is

11. A last summer

   B Last summer

   C Last Summer

   D Correct as it is

12. F Colorado river

   G Colorado River

   H colorado River

   J Correct as it is

(13)   Have you seen the new movie, *cry of the Wolf*? Many scenes were
(14)   filmed on location in yellowstone National Park. The reviewer in the
       Johnson City Times describes it as thrilling.

13. A *Cry Of The Wolf*

   B *Cry of The Wolf*

   C *Cry of the Wolf*

   D Correct as it is

14. F Yellowstone National Park

   G Yellowstone national park

   H yellowstone National park

   J Correct as it is

Assessment continued

Read each set of sentences. Choose the sentence that has correct capitalization.

15. **A** The museum is famous for its collection of chinese pottery.

   B Send your application to P.O. Box 488.

   C My family comes from brazil.

   D Temperatures have been below normal all Month.

16. **F** The shipment is due on Monday.

   G I sent flowers on mother's day.

   H Let's walk on the shady side of the Street.

   J There was an earthquake in Northern California.

17. **A** Pat asked, "who won the game?"

   B There are miles of corn fields in nebraska.

   C Come to the big sale at conway's Department Store!

   D The Indian food at this restaurant is very spicy.

18. **F** The hurricane is headed toward the City of Miami.

   G The class will be taught by professor Lowe.

   H Would you like to subscribe to the *Chicago Tribune*?

   J the traffic is heavy Today.

19. **A** My son joined the cub Scouts.

   B I went to a game at Fenway park.

   C Flights to the Midwest are delayed because of bad weather.

   D Did you recognize uncle Jack?

20. **F** Our hostess said, "your table is ready."

   G She interviewed Mayor Clark.

   H This shop closes at 9:00 p.m.

   J The articles in *People magazine* are always interesting.

21. **A** My Grandmother baked the most delicious chocolate cakes.

   B We made reservations on Banner Airlines.

   C I like to read the jokes in the *reader's digest.*

   D Plant daffodil bulbs in the Fall.

22. **F** The Brooklyn bridge was completed in 1883.

   G We saw the pandas at the San Diego zoo.

   H The umpire yelled, "Strike one!"

   J This letter is for mr. Waldon.

23. **A** Many retired people live in the South.

   B You have to be at least 50 years old to join the Silver dollar club.

   C My brother and i repair old cars.

   D We had a view of the Ocean from our Hotel room.

24. **F** Tina thinks that *What's up, Doc?* is a funny movie.

   G What time does the Bank open?

   H Groundhog day is in February.

   J Volcanoes formed the Hawaiian islands.

End Marks

Period

Use a period at the end of a statement.

> The meeting begins at noon.

Use a period at the end of most commands.

> Turn down the volume.

Question Mark

Use a question mark at the end of a question.

> When is your birthday?

Exclamation Point

Use an exclamation point at the end of an exclamation, that is, a sentence that shows strong feeling, such as excitement or surprise.

> What a great game that was!

Use an exclamation point at the end of a command that expresses a strong or urgent feeling.

> Look out!

Write a period, a question mark, or an exclamation point at the end of each of the following sentences.

1. Park your car in the first space

2. Do you have any experience in sales

3. The Walshes are moving to New Jersey

4. Run for help

5. Fasten your seatbelts

6. What a lot of questions you ask

7. This dessert is so delicious

8. Is the flight going to land on time

9. Hurry up

Practice

Read each of the following pairs of sentences. Choose the sentence with the correct end mark.

1. **A** What a great disguise that is!

   B What a great disguise that is?

2. **A** What kind of shoes did you buy!

   B What kind of shoes did you buy?

3. **A** Tell us another joke.

   B Tell us another joke?

4. **A** My credit card bill is due tomorrow.

   B My credit card bill is due tomorrow?

5. **A** Follow that car!

   B Follow that car?

6. **A** Would you like fries with your meal!

   B Would you like fries with your meal?

Decide which end mark, if any, is needed for each sentence.

7. How many concert tickets did you buy

   A .   **B** ?   **C** !   **D** None

8. Sharon is starting her second year of ballet lessons

   F .   **G** ?   **H** !   **J** None

9. Slow down!

   A .   **B** ?   **C** !   **D** None

10. The party guests shouted, "Surprise"

    F .   **G** ?   **H** !   **J** None

11. Try the vegetable lasagna

    A .   **B** ?   **C** !   **D** None

12. Have you called the repairman yet

    F .   **G** ?   **H** !   **J** None

Apply

Picture yourself in the situations described below. Write a sentence in response to each situation. Use the correct end mark for each sentence.

1. You see a child whose shoes are not tied.

   _____

2. You need directions to the closest convenience store.

   _____

3. You have just seen a really dull movie.

   _____

4. You need to warn someone who is crossing a street that a car is coming.

   _____

5. A friend has just shown you photos of her new baby.

   _____

6. You need to tell an interviewer your birthdate.

   _____

7. You would like to ask a friend to join you for dinner.

   _____

8. You want your son to clean his room.

   _____

9. You are telling someone where you went on your last vacation.

   _____

10. You see a robbery taking place.

   _____

Check Up

Read each set of sentences. Choose the sentence that has the correct end mark.

1. **A** What a beautiful day it is?

   B Check in at Gate C4.

   C Can I help you.

   D My cat's name is Elmo?

2. **F** Show me your driver's license!

   G How brave that man was!

   H Don't touch the hot stove?

   J Crystal rented two movies?

3. **A** Turn left at the next street?

   B What a beautiful necklace.

   C Would you like a hamburger or a hot dog!

   D Stop running in the hallways!

4. **F** Don't tell me how the movie ends?

   G Does anyone know where my car keys are.

   H This room is a mess?

   J You can buy fresh corn at the farmers' market.

5. **A** How much should I tip the waiter?

   B Put the napkins on the table!

   C How noisy that dog is?

   D The envelopes are in the top drawer!

6. **F** What an incredible juggling act that was!

   G What kind of job would you like!

   H The bowling alley closes at midnight?

   J Return your library books?

7. **A** What kind of car do you own.

   B Remember to use sunscreen.

   C How awful that show was?

   D The shipment should arrive tomorrow?

8. **F** Do you have change for a dollar.

   G How cold this water is?

   H Does the price include sales tax?

   J Please pass the mustard?

Decide which end mark is needed for each sentence.

9. This model is our most popular

   A .   **B** ?   **C** !   **D** None

10. I have the winning ticket

    F .   **G** ?   **H** !   **J** None

11. Stand up when your name is called

    A .   **B** ?   **C** !   **D** None

Commas in Compound Sentences

A **compound sentence** is made up of two or more complete sentences, each expressing a complete idea. Each part is called an **independent clause**. Every clause has its own subject and predicate. Two independent clauses often are connected by the words *and, or, nor, but, yet,* or *for.* Place a comma after the first complete thought, before the connecting word.

> The bus is <u>late, and</u> I'm tired of waiting for it.

Do not use a comma if a connecting word such as *and* or *or* connects compound parts of a single sentence.

> Either <u>Damon or Shanti</u> should win the award. (compound subject)
>
> We <u>scraped and sanded</u> the old fence. (compound verb)

Circle the number of each compound sentence that needs a comma. Insert the comma wherever it is needed.

1. Neither the driver nor the passenger saw the exit sign.

2. Do you want to wash dishes or would you prefer to dry them?

3. Ann and Dave went to the art museum but the building was closed.

4. We saw the accident and called for help.

5. Everyone stood at attention for the band was playing the national anthem.

6. Mr. Robb or Ms. Avery will be happy to answer your questions.

7. The plot of the movie was good but the acting was terrible.

8. Larry chopped and stacked all of that wood.

9. No cabs were in sight and the last train had left the station.

10. They left earlier than usual for the traffic was very heavy.

Practice

Read each pair of sentences. Choose the sentence that is written correctly.

1. **A** Doug ordered an SUV, but it hasn't come yet.

   B Doug ordered an SUV but, it hasn't come yet.

2. **A** A boulder broke loose, and tumbled down the hill.

   B A boulder broke loose and tumbled down the hill.

3. **A** She dropped the vase and it crashed to the floor.

   B She dropped the vase, and it crashed to the floor.

4. **A** Either your dog or my cat is responsible for this mess.

   B Either your dog, or my cat is responsible for this mess.

5. **A** I was late this morning, for my car would not start.

   B I was late this morning for, my car would not start.

Read each sentence. Add commas wherever they are needed.

6. Our paper shredder handles large loads but sometimes it jams.

7. The social committee plans all the parties and buys any gifts.

8. Do you want to go for a walk or would you rather rest?

9. I can't stay any longer for it's getting late.

10. Neither the Bensons nor the Smythes have a pet.

11. The work is difficult but the pay is very good.

12. This restaurant is vegetarian and the one next door serves seafood.

13. I can't come today nor can I make it tomorrow.

14. Hikers often use this trail but it is not well marked.

15. A gray whale surfaced and swam near our ship.

Apply

Read each sentence. Add a comma if necessary. Place an **X** over any comma that is used incorrectly. Write **C** on the line if the sentence is punctuated correctly.

1. The house has many good features but it needs some work. _____

2. We can change your oil, or rotate your tires in just a few minutes. _____

3. Neither Bill, nor Sara knew about the pay raise. _____

4. I plan to open my own business, and I intend to succeed. _____

5. Buy this van now for the price won't get any lower. _____

6. The steak was too rare but the lobster was excellent. _____

7. Liz searched thoroughly, but she didn't find her keys. _____

8. There are cabs near the station or you can take a bus into town. _____

9. The garden club replaced the shrubs, and planted new flowers at City Hall. _____

10. Should we get new siding now or should we wait until next year? _____

11. You cannot take pictures in the museum, nor are you permitted to eat or drink. _____

12. Tall trees, and shrubs hid the house from view. _____

13. We gasped in fear for our raft nearly tipped over in the swirling water. _____

14. Phil, and his dog camped in the wilderness for a month. _____

15. Side streets were clogged with snow, but the main streets had been cleared. _____

Read each pair of sentences. Choose the sentence that is punctuated correctly.

16. **A** Joe went home, and watched television.

    B Joe went home and watched television.

17. **A** Donna visited her grandmother, and Therese saw the art exhibit.

    B Donna visited her grandmother and Therese saw the art exhibit.

18. **A** The hotel room was run-down, but its view of the river was beautiful.

    B The hotel room was run-down but its view of the river was beautiful.

Check Up

Read each group of sentences. Choose the sentence that is punctuated correctly.

1. **A** Aunt Mae intended to knit the afghan, but she crocheted it instead.

   B She designed, and sewed the quilt herself.

   C Helen, or Bob can take your order.

   D Is dinner ready or, will we have to wait longer?

2. **F** Either the TV, or the VCR is not working.

   G The beach was crowded and the sand was too hot.

   H He pressed the suit carefully, and hung it on a hanger.

   J Henry loves to travel, but his wife would rather stay home.

3. **A** My older son, and I spent the day at the zoo.

   B Shirley canned or, froze all the vegetables from the garden.

   C We were glad Mel won the promotion, for we knew how hard he had worked for it.

   D The day was gloomy and the rain made everyone grumpy.

4. **F** Do you have cash or, will you write a check?

   G The jury left the courtroom, and the judge went to her chambers.

   H Grandmother reads, or knits every afternoon.

   J We tried to park the car but the lot was full.

Read each sentence and look at the underlined part. Choose the answer that is written correctly for the underlined part.

5. Louise is <u>tall but</u>, Lynn is even taller.

   A tall but

   B tall, but

   C tall, but,

   D Correct as it is

6. We heard a cracking <u>noise and</u> then a tree limb fell to the <u>ground</u>.

   F noise, and

   G noise and,

   H noise, and,

   J Correct as it is

7. The radio was very <u>loud, for</u> someone had reset the <u>volume</u>.

   A loud for

   B loud for,

   C loud, for,

   D Correct as it is

8. <u>Ants, and</u> flies ruined our picnic.

   F Ants and,

   G Ants, and,

   H Ants and

   J Correct as it is

Commas in Complex Sentences

A **complex sentence** is made up of one independent clause and one or more **dependent clauses** (which can't stand alone). The dependent clause is joined to the main clause by a connecting word like *although*, *because*, *if*, *when*, or *that*.

When the dependent clause comes at the start of the sentence, put a comma after it and before the independent clause.

    When the hawk flew over his head, Jerry ducked.

When the dependent clause comes at the end of the sentence, don't use a comma.

    Jerry ducked when the hawk flew over his head.

Circle the number of each complex sentence that needs a comma. Insert the comma wherever it is needed.

1. Although it's after nine at night it's still light out.

2. If the shoe fits wear it.

3. It's a sure thing that Mr. Jenkins will say no.

4. As soon as you hear anything let me know.

5. The bell will ring if the lab rat chooses the right path.

6. When Ms. Chen saw the mess the kids had made she was furious.

7. John tracked mud into the kitchen after Tom washed the floor.

8. Because the manual was useless Don couldn't get the computer to work.

9. Unless Carla returns my car by five o'clock I'm never lending it to her again.

10. The whole town celebrated because it was Independence Day.

11. As Ricky drove down the hill he hit a patch of ice.

12. The check will be late because I forgot to mail it.

Practice

Read each pair of sentences. Choose the sentence that is written correctly.

1. **A** If you think that's bad you should see the other movie.

   B If you think that's bad, you should see the other movie.

2. **A** Elaine told Greg not to come back until he was ready to apologize.

   B Elaine told Greg not to come back, until he was ready to apologize.

3. **A** I'm here because I want to buy a book.

   B I'm here, because I want to buy a book.

4. **A** When I called Pam she refused to talk to me.

   B When I called Pam, she refused to talk to me.

5. **A** Leni has been good at math since she was very young.

   B Leni has been good at math, since she was very young.

Read each sentence. Add commas wherever they are needed.

6. As the wind blew harder the walls of the house creaked.

7. Shirley got to class before the bell rang.

8. If you go outside just before sunrise you'll see Venus above the crescent moon.

9. Although it's almost November we haven't had a killing frost yet.

10. Sam picked the roses while Jan picked the tomatoes.

11. Ever since George failed his test he's been studying harder.

12. Sally learned to fly when she served in the Air Force.

13. When the plane landed John was waiting.

14. After they took a brief intermission the band started playing again.

15. Unless Jack sets his alarm he'll be late for work.

16. Wherever Merrill hides her dog will find her.

Apply

Read each sentence. Add a comma if necessary. Place an _X_ over any comma that is used incorrectly. Write _C_ on the line if the sentence is punctuated correctly.

1. Lynn has wanted to be her own boss, as long as she can remember. _____

2. She decided to become a tax preparer, because she likes numbers. _____

3. Even when her taxes were complicated she always did them herself. _____

4. As a first step she asked the Small Business Administration for help. _____

5. A mentor taught her, what she needed to know about writing a business plan.

6. He advised her not to take out a bank loan until she saw how business went. _____

7. While taking a class she learned about the different tax forms. _____

8. After Lynn graduated, she was ready to go out on her own. _____

9. She set up her office in her living room because she couldn't afford extra rent. _____

10. At first, only a few relatives and friends were her clients. _____

11. Soon however, word got out that Lynn was good at her job. _____

12. Since she found ways to save money for her clients they were happy. _____

13. If she pleased one client two more would show up. _____

14. She made time for everyone, except those few who wanted her to cheat. _____

15. Lynn wanted to take a vacation, but she was too busy. _____

Read each pair of sentences. Choose the sentence that is punctuated correctly.

16. **A** As Ron balanced his checkbook, he began to feel nervous.

    B As Ron balanced his checkbook he began to feel nervous.

17. **A** You'll be running a marathon, before you know it.

    B You'll be running a marathon before you know it.

18. **A** If I train for six months, I might be able to run six miles.

    B If I train for six months I might be able to run six miles.

Check Up

Read each group of sentences. Choose the sentence that is punctuated correctly.

1. **A** When you recite poetry out loud, it can be good for your health.

   B The benefits happen, because reciting makes your heart beat in time with your breath.

   C Usually you breathe 15 times per minute but your blood pressure has 10-second cycles.

   D In fact synchronizing may improve your lungs.

2. **F** Because she expected a hard winter, Marge winterized her house.

   G First she put caulking, around all the windows.

   H Then she bought insulated curtains, although they were expensive.

   J Finally she insulated the exterior walls, because they were always cold.

3. **A** When humans first landed on the moon Nixon was president.

   B Neil Armstrong is remembered today, because he was the first person to walk on the moon.

   C When the astronauts went to the moon, they brought back moon rocks.

   D They brought back more than 800 pounds of rocks, so that scientists could learn more about the moon.

4. **F** Although butterflies need freedom you can raise them in your garden.

   G If you like butterflies, plant a refuge for them.

   H Plant parsley and dill because caterpillars like them.

   J They like bee balm and phlox, after they become butterflies.

Read each sentence and look at the underlined part. Choose the answer that is written correctly for the underlined part.

5. The moon <u>rose before</u>, dark last night.

   A rose, before

   B rose, before,

   C rose before

   D Correct as it is

6. Since Tom left his <u>job, he's been</u> self-employed.

   F job he's, been

   G job he's been,

   H job he's been

   J Correct as it is

7. While Juan did the <u>dishes Luna fed</u> the cats.

   A dishes, Luna fed

   B dishes Luna, fed

   C dishes Luna fed,

   D Correct as it is

8. Louise Nevelson became an <u>artist, because she</u> loved shapes.

   F artist because, she

   G artist because she,

   H artist because she

   J Correct as it is

Commas in Series

Use commas to separate the members in a series of three or more words or short phrases. Place commas after each word or phrase in the series except the last one.

> Cars, buses, and trucks jammed the freeway.
>
> We will camp in the mountains, go to the beach, or stay home for our vacation.
>
> What a cold, snowy, miserable day it is!

Do not use commas if all of the words or phrases in the series are joined by connecting words.

> Buy ice cream or sherbert or frozen yogurt when you shop.

Read each of the following items and add commas wherever they are needed. If a phrase does not need a comma, write *Correct* on the line.

1. guppies goldfish and tiger barbs _____

2. shook shuddered and collapsed _____

3. piles of magazines stacks of books and mounds of papers

   _____

4. Mr. Berg Ms. Allen or Dr. Pike _____

5. phlox and daisies and marigolds _____

6. hot tangy and satisfying _____

7. mowed the lawn trimmed the bushes and watered the flowers

   _____

8. Boston or New York or Atlanta _____

9. the dentist her assistant and the hygienist _____

10. swayed clapped or danced _____

Practice

Read each pair of sentences. Choose the sentence in which commas are used correctly.

1. **A** Is Dr. Willis, Dr. Bradford or Dr. Vizquel, skilled in that procedure?

   B Is Dr. Willis, Dr. Bradford, or Dr. Vizquel skilled in that procedure?

2. **A** The market sold fresh fruit, many vegetables, and cut flowers.

   B The market sold fresh fruit, many vegetables and cut flowers.

3. **A** We sanded, floors stained, woodwork and painted, walls.

   B We sanded floors, stained woodwork, and painted walls.

4. **A** Tall sedges, lacy ferns, and colorful hostas, surrounded the pond.

   B Tall sedges, lacy ferns, and colorful hostas surrounded the pond.

5. **A** Pink, red, yellow, and white flowers dotted the hillside.

   B Pink, red, yellow and white, flowers dotted the hillside.

Read each sentence. Add commas wherever necessary. Write _C_ on the line if the sentence is correct as it is.

6. Please copy these pages collate the copies and place the papers in a binder. _____

7. Aaron had an angry sullen belligerent look on his face. _____

8. Does the deli serve soup dessert or a beverage with the meal? _____

9. Horses sheep and cattle are bought and sold at the Auction Barn. _____

10. Bring your own dishes silverware and side dish for the potluck. _____

11. Neither Lou nor Kate nor Molly wanted that job. _____

12. Settlers traveled by foot on horseback or in wagons to their new homes. _____

13. Contact Maurice Jack or Abdul for your banking needs. _____

14. Should we visit a museum tour the monuments or browse through the shops today? _____

15. The freeway was a maze of orange barrels detour signs and construction equipment. _____

Apply

Rewrite each of the following sentences, placing commas wherever they are needed. If the sentence is correct as it is, write *Correct* on the line.

1. It was a hot hazy sultry day.

   _____

2. Jerry Laurie Don and Phyllis went to the air show.

   _____

3. Clap your hands stamp your feet and twirl your partner.

   _____

4. Rabbits gray squirrels and deer made their homes in the forest.

   _____

5. Will you plant wheat or rye or oats this year?

   _____

6. Seagulls circled swooped low and gently landed on the water.

   _____

7. Buy tuna steaks fresh shrimp or whitefish fillets for dinner.

   _____

8. The tour bus stops at Hoover Dam the Grand Canyon and Four Corners.

   _____

9. Will a birdbath a trellis or a bench look best in the garden?

   _____

10. I'll have mushrooms and peppers and sausage on my pizza.

   _____

Check Up

Read each set of sentences. Choose the sentence in which commas are used correctly.

1. **A** Oak, poplar, and spruce, trees surrounded the house.

   B Huge, ugly, red, blotches covered his hands.

   C Does ragweed, grass or tree pollen make you sneeze?

   D The bouquet contains roses, lilies, and hyacinths.

2. **F** The hay was cut dried, and packed in huge bundles.

   G Stan tripped stumbled and fell, on the uneven sidewalk.

   H Insert the key, turn the dial, and start the machine.

   J Unruly fans pushed shoved and elbowed, their way to the exits.

3. **A** We'll finish eighth, ninth, or tenth in the race.

   B I'll have one, or two, or three cookies for dessert.

   C The teams in first, second and third, place are in the play-offs.

   D Our flight is delayed until noon one o'clock, or later.

4. **F** Max Wendy and Jeff, work for the same company.

   G My brothers live in Ohio, Virginia, and Oregon.

   H The village contained a clinic, a few shops, and, a restaurant.

   J Maury may travel to Mexico, Puerto Rico, or Peru, this fall.

Read each sentence and look at the underlined part. Choose the answer that is written correctly for the underlined part.

5. Are you looking for an <u>SUV, a minivan or a truck</u>, today?

   A SUV, a minivan, or a truck

   B SUV a minivan or a truck

   C SUV, a minivan, or, a truck

   D Correct as it is

6. The storm arrived with peals of <u>thunder lightning and hail</u>.

   F thunder, lightning and hail

   G thunder, lightning, and hail

   H thunder, lightning and, hail

   J Correct as it is

7. Please <u>turn off the lights, lock the door, and leave the key at the desk</u>.

   A turn off the lights lock the door, and leave the key at the desk

   B turn off the lights, lock the door, and, leave the key at the desk

   C turn off the lights, lock the door and leave the key at the desk

   D Correct as it is

8. We were greeted warmly by a <u>tall, kindly white-haired</u> gentleman.

   F tall, kindly, white-haired

   G tall, kindly white-haired

   H tall, kindly, white-haired,

   J Correct as it is

Commas with Appositives

A **appositive** is a word or phrase added to a sentence to explain or rename another word. An appositive means the same thing as the word it explains. Use commas to set off an appositive from the rest of the sentence.

> Tanya Hoffman, a master carpenter, built a deck.

> Allison, the president of the civic club, gave a speech.

If a term such as *or*, *namely*, or *also known as* introduces the appositive, include it inside the commas.

> The tulip tree, or yellow poplar, is a beautiful tree.

If a renaming phrase comes before the word it explains, it's an adjective phrase, not an appositive. It should not be set off with commas.

> Master carpenter Tanya Hoffman built a deck.

Underline the appositive in each sentence. Draw an arrow to the word the appositive explains.

1. William Shakespeare, the playwright, was born in 1564.

2. Aphra Behn, an Englishwoman, wrote some of the first English novels.

3. Bob watched his favorite team, the Steelers, win the championship.

4. H.H. Munro, or Saki, is known for his short stories.

5. Hyacinths, my favorite flowers, smell wonderful.

Use an appositive from the list and complete each sentence. Place commas correctly.

my neighbors	the supervisor
the electrician	the Salinger twins
the quilters	a top student

6. Fran and Chloe _____.

7. Ignatz Smith _____.

8. Bill Jones _____.

9. Pauli and Dennis _____.

10. Tony O'Brien _____.

Practice

Underline the appositive in each sentence. Place commas wherever they are needed.

1. The house, a two-story Colonial, sold quickly.

2. My grandmother, a member of the Cree tribe, is a wise woman.

3. Asteroids, an old video game, was good for hand-eye coordination.

4. Idlewild, the oldest amusement park in the area, has a wooden roller coaster.

5. Rose of Sharon, or tree of heaven, is a flowering shrub.

6. Liberal candidate Chris Goldstein won the election.

7. Bessie Smith, the empress of the blues, sang "St. Louis Woman."

8. Charles Windsor, the Prince of Wales, has two children.

9. Famous architect Frank Lloyd Wright designed Fallingwater.

10. The cheetah, the fastest land animal in the world, can outrun a car.

Read each sentence. Add commas wherever necessary.

11. That stone, a gray striped rock, is a million years old.

12. Professional musician Ray Davies was a member of the Kinks.

13. Physics, my favorite subject, covers the interaction of matter and energy.

14. December 21, the winter solstice, is the shortest day of the year.

15. Either vinyl or tile flooring will work well in the kitchen.

16. Hank Aaron, a star batter, is in the Baseball Hall of Fame.

17. I take the subway, a convenient mode of transport, every day.

18. *Rudbeckia*, namely brown-eyed Susan, is a colorful flower.

19. Michael Jordan, a forward, played for the Chicago Bulls.

Apply

Rewrite each sentence. Add commas wherever they are needed.

1. Danielle's husband Roberto often travels to Argentina.

_____

2. Sam's only daughter Elayne graduated from the University of Pittsburgh.

_____

3. Wolfgang is very good at playing his favorite instrument the flute.

_____

4. The red maple tree also known as _acer rubrum_ has very colorful leaves in the fall.

_____

5. Committee chair Frances Burns called the meeting to order.

_____

6. Eliza Habera the mayor of Mt. Pleasant plans to run for state senator.

_____

7. Chickpeas also known as garbanzo beans are nutritious.

_____

8. Ahmed Akbar an antiques dealer is an expert in illuminated manuscripts.

_____

9. Olympic swimmer Amanda Beard won several medals in 2004.

_____

10. Simone de Beauvoir a leading existentialist was born in 1908.

_____

Check Up

Read each sentence. Choose the answer whose underlined part is written correctly.

1. James <u>Joyce a pioneer</u> of stream of consciousness, wrote *Ulysses*.
   - **A** Joyce, a pioneer
   - **B** Joyce, a pioneer,
   - **C** Joyce a pioneer,
   - **D** Correct as it is

2. My insurance <u>company, Maintain Health,</u> raised my premium.
   - **F** company Maintain Health
   - **G** company, Maintain Health
   - **H** company Maintain Health,
   - **J** Correct as it is

3. Nobel Peace Prize <u>winner Rigoberta Menchu</u> is from Guatemala.
   - **A** winner, Rigoberta Menchu
   - **B** winner, Rigoberta Menchu,
   - **C** winner Rigoberta Menchu,
   - **D** Correct as it is

4. I ran into Ms. <u>Lightfoot my algebra teacher,</u> at the mall.
   - **F** Lightfoot my algebra teacher
   - **G** Lightfoot, my algebra teacher
   - **H** Lightfoot, my algebra teacher,
   - **J** Correct as it is

Read each group of sentences. Choose the sentence that is punctuated correctly.

5.
   - **A** Marie Curie, the discoverer of radium, won two Nobel Prizes.
   - **B** She and her husband Pierre shared the prize in 1903.
   - **C** Curie a Polish scientist studied in Paris.
   - **D** A physics professor, at the Sorbonne Curie died in 1934.

6.
   - **F** Carbon dioxide or CO_2 is the main cause of global warming.
   - **G** Carbon dioxide forms carbonic acid a weak acid, in water.
   - **H** Carbonic acid damages shellfish, fish that need calcium to make their shells.
   - **J** CO_2 is released by the burning of coal and oil or fossil fuels.

7.
   - **A** Mary Ann Evans also known as George Eliot wrote *Middlemarch*.
   - **B** She was the youngest child of Robert Evans an estate agent.
   - **C** Her writing was admired by Victoria, the queen of England.
   - **D** Her work was praised by Virginia Woolf author of *Orlando*.

8.
   - **F** Blood the river of life, runs through your body.
   - **G** Eurythrocytes, the red cells are the most abundant cells in the blood.
   - **H** Platelets also known as thrombocytes are the smallest blood cells.
   - **J** Your coronary, or heart, arteries pump blood through your body.

Other Uses of Commas

Sentences sometimes begin with a word or phrase that is not part of the subject. Commas make such sentences easier to understand.

Put a comma after *yes* or *no* at the beginning of a sentence if the word is used to answer a question or to make a comment.

> <u>Yes</u>, this is my photo album of my trip to Spain.

Use a comma after a long phrase that begins a sentence to separate it from the rest of the sentence.

> <u>Walking quickly down Main Street</u>, Mario arrived at our favorite café.

Short phrases of four words or less need a comma only if the sentence is hard to understand without it.

> <u>By the way</u>, I just noticed a scratch on the bumper.
> By daybreak John was hard at work.

Choose the sentence in each pair in which commas are used correctly.

1. **A** No, my dog was not barking all night.

   B No my dog, was not barking all night.

2. **A** To reach, the top shelf use the step stool.

   B To reach the top shelf, use the step stool.

3. **A** Yes I talked to Walter yesterday.

   B Yes, I talked to Walter yesterday.

4. **A** During dinner they talked over the day's events.

   B During dinner, they talked over the day's events.

5. **A** Pedaling furiously, the bicyclist climbed the steep hill.

   B Pedaling, furiously the bicyclist climbed the steep hill.

Practice

Use commas for the following situations:

If someone or something is directly addressed, set off the name of the person or thing with commas. In the examples below, commas are used to set off **words of direct address** at the beginning, end, and middle of sentences.

Grandmother, it's so good to see you!

Please follow me, Mrs. Stebbins.

Fetch the newspaper, Rover, and bring it to me.

When the names of a **city** and a **state** are part of a sentence, place a comma between them.

The Space Needle is in Seattle, Washington.

Circle the word or words of direct address in each sentence.

1. Do you have any homework, son?

2. Finish your dinner, Mike, before you mow the lawn.

3. Dr. Blackburn, your office called.

4. Thank you, sweetheart, for the candy.

5. We'll miss you, Sandy.

Read each sentence. Add commas wherever necessary.

6. Judge Thomas may I speak with you?

7. Diane and her family moved to Tucson Arizona.

8. No I haven't seen the newspaper Stephanie.

9. By this time tomorrow we should reach Omaha Nebraska.

10. Please leave the theater ladies and gentlemen by the doors to your left.

11. By exercising every day Roberto hopes to regain his strength.

12. Before going on to Japan the plane refueled in Honolulu Hawaii.

13. Leaping into the air Lonnie caught the fly ball.

14. Yes Pamela the computer is working again.

Apply

Rewrite each of the following sentences. Add commas wherever they are needed.

1. Yes the tour bus stops in New Orleans Louisiana.

   _____

2. According to the map we should have gotten off at the last exit Stan.

   _____

3. In time William will understand.

   _____

4. No Nick this is not the CD you wanted.

   _____

5. If you need fuel Dolly stop at the next service station.

   _____

6. Glittering in the sun the spiderweb was breathtaking.

   _____

7. Shortly after graduating from college Beth moved to Denver Colorado.

   _____

8. Without the remote control Kurt nobody can change channels.

   _____

9. At dawn they began the long trek to Arches National Park near Moab Utah.

   _____

10. Weak from exhaustion Greta stepped across the finish line.

   _____

Check Up

Read each set of sentences. Choose the sentence in which commas are used correctly.

1. **A** Tonya visited her family in, Newark New Jersey.

   B After the long drought the rain, was welcome.

   C Yes, the item you ordered has been sent.

   D Tell us sir, your thoughts on city government.

2. **F** Wagging its tail, the dog barked a friendly "hello."

   G Vivian what have you decided to do about the problem?

   H No Henry, the car is not available right now.

   J Our goal was to reach Miami Florida, by nightfall.

3. **A** Yes, several appointments are open, Dr. Chang.

   B Dodging the traffic, Eddie, sprinted across the street.

   C At dusk fireflies flickered, around the yard.

   D By the way is it too late, to make a reservation for tonight?

4. **F** Ms. Gomez please return to the information booth.

   G Yes, Mr. Johnston, will be attending the business conference.

   H Get on the Blue Ridge Parkway at Front Royal, Virginia.

   J After searching through his pockets, Lee, found the tickets.

Read each sentence and look at the underlined part. Choose the answer that is written correctly for the underlined part.

5. When you complete the <u>measurements, Mr. Wells, will you give me an estimate?</u>

   A measurements, Mr. Wells

   B measurements Mr. Wells,

   C measurements Mr. Wells

   D Correct as it is

6. No, the state capital is <u>not Detroit Michigan</u>.

   F not Detroit, Michigan

   G not, Detroit, Michigan

   H not, Detroit Michigan

   J Correct as it is

7. With their exciting <u>performance the chorus</u>, soon had the audience singing along.

   A performance, the chorus,

   B performance, the chorus

   C performance the chorus

   D Correct as it is

8. <u>Yes, Mr. Brown</u> the job is finished.

   F Yes Mr. Brown,

   G Yes, Mr. Brown,

   H Yes Mr. Brown

   J Correct as it is

Semicolons and Colons

Use a **semicolon** between clauses in a compound
sentence if no conjunction is used.

> The plane taxied down the runway; it picked
> up speed.
>
> Katherine knew that the test would be difficult;
> she was determined to pass it.

Insert a semicolon in the correct place in each sentence.

1. It was a cold spring some of the flowers didn't bloom at all.

2. Ben knew that the operation was simple it only lasted an hour.

3. We painted our house red, white, and blue it looks like the American flag.

4. The phone rang in the middle of the night it was a wrong number.

5. Jane found pictures of her aunt Edith they were in a box in the attic.

6. The roads leading away from the city were crowded it seemed that everyone wanted to get away for the weekend.

7. It had not rained for weeks the ground was cracked and dry.

8. Two runners had finished the race together they were both given first prize.

9. The fast-food place offers large, extra-large, and giant burgers they are served on sesame seed buns.

10. The printer has run out of paper can you tell me where to find more?

11. The computer is five years old it is an out-of-date model.

12. Rebecca put a picture on her desk it is of her parents on their wedding day.

13. They are tearing down a whole block of buildings new condominiums will go up next fall.

14. Debbie keeps a journal she writes in it every night before she goes to bed.

Practice

Use a **colon** to introduce a list of items. Before the colon, identify the type of list to be named. The words *these*, *the following*, or a number indicate that a list will follow.

> **Correct:** The modern pentathlon has these events: horseback riding, fencing, running, swimming, and shooting.

> **Incorrect:** The modern pentathlon has: horseback riding, fencing, running, swimming, and shooting.

Use a colon between numerals that tell the hour and the minute.

> The flight will depart at 7:35 P.M.

Read each of the following pairs of sentences. Choose the sentence that uses semicolons and colons correctly.

1. **A** Be sure to pack these items: pajamas, a toothbrush, and toothpaste.

   B Be sure to pack these items; pajamas, a toothbrush, and toothpaste.

2. **A** I visited these cities: Houston, St. Louis, and Springfield.

   B I visited: Houston, St. Louis, and Springfield.

3. **A** The movie begins at 8:10 P.M.

   B The movie begins at 8;10 P.M.

4. **A** The restaurant was ugly: the color of the walls clashed with the pattern of the chairs.

   B The restaurant was ugly; the color of the walls clashed with the pattern of the chairs.

Read each sentence. Add a semicolon or a colon wherever necessary. Place an *X* over any semicolon or colon that is used incorrectly.

5. We have ham, cheese, and chicken sandwiches they were prepared this morning.

6. My grandfather was born in: Bay City, Michigan.

7. Suzanne wants to be a professional model she has even hired an agent to handle her business.

8. To make my special salad, I need these ingredients lettuce, bean sprouts, raspberries, and sliced almonds.

Apply

Rewrite each of the following sentences. Add semicolons and colons wherever they are needed.

1. David sent out more than fifty applications he finally got a good job.

   _____

2. The audience rose and applauded wildly the singers returned many times for bows.

   _____

3. The storeroom has pens, paper, and staples it has no notebooks.

   _____

4. Success requires three things skill, patience, and persistence.

   _____

5. Heather sorted glass and plastic from cardboard and paper she thinks that it is important to recycle.

   _____

6. Our baby boy was born at 312 A.M. on Tuesday.

   _____

7. The mailman came at 1030 he delivered three catalogs.

   _____

8. I never expected to win I almost didn't enter the contest.

   _____

9. The tour will visit these cities Rome, Paris, and London.

   _____

10. Diane works well with the people in her office she hopes to become manager.

    _____

Check Up

Read each group of sentences. Choose the sentence that is punctuated correctly.

1. **A** These dances will be taught: the jitterbug, the foxtrot, and the waltz.

    B I left the building at 7;30 P.M.

    C The judge entered the courtroom; and everyone stopped talking.

    D Marcia is doing well: she got a promotion.

2. **F** The bus is usually on time: today it's late.

    G Our yard has: elm trees, fir trees, and maple trees.

    H Ed's car is a lemon; he can't wait to get rid of it.

    J The costumes were great: the movie was dull.

3. **A** The copier is broken: we're waiting for the repairman.

    B I could eat out at breakfast; lunch; and dinner.

    C The orchestra will play works by these composers: Bach, Mozart, and Beethoven.

    D Those capital cities are: Columbus, Sacramento, and Boise.

4. **F** I need a new cell phone; I dropped mine once too often.

    G The roast was in the oven too long, it tastes dry.

    H The reporter asked these questions; who, what, and when.

    J Ann likes peaches, pears, and apples, she loves plums.

Read each sentence and look at the underlined part. Choose the answer that is written correctly for the underlined part.

5. Skydiving is a dangerous <u>sport,</u> many people like it.

    A sport,

    B sport;

    C sport:

    D Correct as it is

6. The following sports will be <u>offered</u>: swimming, baseball, and tennis.

    F offered,

    G offered;

    H offered.

    J Correct as it is

7. The meeting will begin at <u>9;30 A.M.</u> in the conference room.

    A 9:30 A.M.

    B 9.30 A.M.

    C 9,30 A:M:

    D Correct as it is

8. The state fair was a <u>success, new</u> attendance records <u>were set.</u>

    F success: new

    G success. new

    H success; new

    J Correct as it is

Review

End Marks

Place a **period** after a statement or a command. Use a **question mark** to end a question. Put an **exclamation point** at the end of a sentence that expresses excitement or strong feeling.

Commas

Use a comma in the following ways:

- to separate independent clauses joined by a connecting word in a compound sentence. Connecting words include *and, or, nor, but,* and *for.*
- to separate a dependent clause at the beginning of a complex sentence from the independent clause. Connecting words include *although, because, if, when,* and *that.*
- to separate words or phrases written in a series of three or more when no connecting words join the pairs of words or phrases
- to set off an appositive (a word or phrase added to a sentence to explain or rename another word)
- to separate introductory words like *yes* or *no* from the rest of the sentence
- to set off certain short phrases and all long phrases that begin a sentence
- to set off the name of a person or thing being spoken to in a sentence
- to separate the name of a city from its state

Semicolons

Use a **semicolon** in a compound sentence to separate independent clauses that are not joined by a connecting words.

Colons

Use a **colon** to introduce a list of items. Also, place a colon between numerals that name the hour and the minute.

Assessment

Read the following paragraphs and look at their numbered, underlined parts. Choose the answer that is written correctly for each underlined part.

(1)   Ancient <u>Inca, and</u> Pueblo people are noted for the beautiful
(2)   pottery they <u>made.</u> They <u>molded and shaped</u> bowls and other objects
(3)   from clay. Their artistry is admired to this <u>day,</u>

1. **A** Inca and;

    B Inca, and,

    C Inca and

    D Correct as it is

2. **F** molded, and shaped

    G molded, and, shaped

    H molded and shaped:

    J Correct as it is

3. **A** day.

    B day?

    C day;

    D Correct as it is

(4)   Many people like astronomy. With the help of a <u>telescope</u>
(5)   they <u>study:</u> the moon, nearby planets, and stars. Sometimes
(6)   a comet or a meteor <u>shower or</u> a shooting star appears in the sky.
(7)   What an exciting event <u>that is.</u>

4. **F** telescope,

    G telescope.

    H telescope!

    J Correct as it is

5. **A** study

    B study,

    C study;

    D Correct as it is

6. **F** shower or,

    G shower, or,

    H shower, or

    J Correct as it is

7. **A** that is?

    B that is,

    C that is!

    D Correct as it is

(8)   A major transportation center in the Midwest is <u>Chicago Illinois</u>. Most
(9)   people are aware of its bustling <u>airport</u>; it is a hub for train and bus
(10) travel as well. <u>Yes</u> Chicago is a busy city.

8. **F** Chicago; Illinois.

    G Chicago, Illinois,

    H Chicago, Illinois.

    J Correct as it is

10. **F** Yes!

    G Yes,

    H Yes.

    J Correct as it is

9. **A** airport,

    B airport:

    C airport

    D Correct as it is

Decide which mark, if any, is needed in each sentence.

11. What a massive dog that is

    A ?   **B** ,   **C** !   **D** None

12. Are those baskets for sale or are they for display only?

    F ,   **G** ;   **H** :   **J** None

13. Before making that decision think about the consequences.

    A .   **B** ,   **C** ;   **D** None

14. Lou, where are the clippers

    F .   **G** ?   **H** !   **J** None

15. A bank is located in this building now it is closed.

    A ;   **B** ,   **C** :   **D** None

16. Use the stairs for the escalator is not working.

    F ;   **G** ,   **H** :   **J** None

17. Basil and chives add new taste to foods; they are also easy to grow.

    A ;   **B** ,   **C** :   **D** None

Read each group of sentences. Choose the sentence that has correct punctuation.

18. F Are these your glasses Dr. Webb?

    G With great effort we pushed the car to the side of the road.

    H Yes the barbershop opens at 10:15.

    J Would you like tea or coffee or a soft drink?

19. A We inventoried these items: staplers, binders, notecards, and shredders.

    B The cereal contained these ingredients wheat bran, raisins, nuts, and figs.

    C Ms. Patel your table is ready.

    D Have you found your credit card!

20. F The walls were lined with plush velvet; shiny moire; and silk.

    G Bill, and Pete ran the 10K race.

    H After lunch we traveled to Savannah, Georgia.

    J Conferences were held in these cities Ely, Columbus, and Lakewood.

21. A After Leah sanded the rough spots she varnished the floor.

    B When Ng was promoted, everyone congratulated him.

    C Delia plans to start training, in the spring.

    D If the meeting is held at 4:00 P.M. Ms. Tan, Mr. Munn, and Dr. Lewis can all attend it.

22. F The interior was not painted nor was the tile laid on the floor?

    G A bus departs for Buffalo at these times: 11:15, 2:45, and 7:20.

    H Yes, sir your car has been repaired.

    J Manuevering carefully; the crane operator lifted the heavy load.

23. A The farmers' market sold corn, and potatoes, and beans.

    B Alice had a table; Jeff provided the chairs.

    C Why is the traffic moving so slowly.

    D Ali asked, "How far are you traveling today, Phil."

24. F Eric pursues his favorite exercise biking, every weekend.

    G Dorothy's camera, a Leica is an antique.

    H The river, always unpredictable, overran its banks during the storm.

    J Jane's favorite TV show a sitcom is on Thursday nights.

25. A A bear: ambled through our camp, searched our tent, and took our food!

    B No, Professor Grenfeld, does not teach that class.

    C Order the siding now Bill; wait until later to buy the shutters.

    D Frankly, Kim, it's not possible to change the appointment.

Writing Quotations

A **direct quotation** is the exact words of a speaker. When you write a direct quotation, enclose the speaker's words in quotation marks (" "). Do not put quotation marks around words that identify the speaker.

Include the end mark for the quotation inside the quotation marks. Capitalize the first word of a direct quotation.

> The angry customer demanded, "Give me back my money!"

An **indirect quotation** repeats a speaker's message but does not use the speaker's exact words. Do not enclose indirect quotations in quotation marks.

Indirect: The clerk advised her to go to Customer Service.

Direct: The clerk advised her, "Go to Customer Service."

Add quotation marks wherever they are needed in each sentence. If the sentence is an indirect quotation, write *IQ* on the line.

1. _____ The usher mumbled, Go to the theater on the left.

2. _____ My sister said that unless I hurried, I would miss the bus.

3. _____ Where is the petite department? Karla asked the clerk.

4. _____ Our neighbor complained that our dog was keeping him up at night.

5. _____ Let's leave now! whispered Leeann.

6. _____ Vince asked, Which late-night show is your favorite?

7. _____ The frightened woman cried, My house is on fire!

8. _____ The officer reported that the situation was under control.

9. _____ Claudia suggested that we could take a bus to the museum.

10. _____ Run for home! Matt shouted.

11. _____ Mrs. O'Connor insisted that her idea would work.

12. _____ Jordan said, I am finally getting used to decaf coffee.

Practice

When you write direct quotations, remember these capitalization and punctuation rules:

- If the phrase that identifies the speaker comes before the quotation, place a comma after the phrase and before the quotation marks.

    Lee asked, "What will we have for dinner?"

- If the quotation is a statement, and it comes before the phrase that identifies the speaker, use a comma instead of a period as its end mark.

    "I'm going to the grocery store now," said Elena.

- Enclose both parts of a divided quotation in quotation marks. Do not capitalize the second part unless it begins a new sentence.

    "Wait just a minute," said Lee, "and I'll join you."

    "That would be nice," replied Elena. "We can walk there."

Read each of the following pairs of sentences. Choose the sentence that is capitalized and punctuated correctly.

1. **A** The astronaut exclaimed "planet Earth looks beautiful!"

    B The astronaut exclaimed, "Planet Earth looks beautiful!"

2. **A** "What I hate about bowling said Niki, is wearing someone else's shoes."

    B "What I hate about bowling," said Niki, "is wearing someone else's shoes."

3. **A** "Is anyone taking notes?" asked the chairperson.

    B "Is anyone taking notes"? asked the chairperson.

4. **A** "Let's go out for dinner," suggested Amy.

    B "Let's go out for dinner." suggested Amy.

5. **A** The injured player said that he was feeling better.

    B The injured player said "that he was feeling better."

6. **A** "My brother lives in Houston," said Carol. "he's visiting us for a week."

    B "My brother lives in Houston," said Carol. "He's visiting us for a week."

Apply

Read each of the following sentences. Add commas wherever they are needed. (One sentence needs no commas added to it.)

1. The librarian said "Please be quiet in the library."

2. "I can proofread your letter" offered Ruth.

3. "My baby sleeps all day" complained Teresa "and is awake all night."

4. "Have you ever seen this movie before?" asked Tim.

5. The night watchman shouted "Stay where you are!"

6. "Our goal" said the director "is to please every customer."

Read each sentence. If it is capitalized and punctuated correctly, write *Correct* on the line. If not, rewrite the sentence correctly.

7. Marla asked, would you like a second helping?

_____

8. The driver says that I owe another dollar.

_____

9. My computer crashed again! whined Bobbi.

_____

10. Gabe said "I like strawberries in my cereal,"

_____

11. "This summer is hot, admitted Jon, but last summer was hotter."

_____

12. "Our team," complained the coach, "is getting too many penalties".

_____

13. Aaron asked? "Have you heard any good jokes lately"

_____

14. "I run two miles every morning." said Michelle.

_____

Check Up

Read each group of sentences. Choose the sentence that is written correctly.

1. A Valerie wailed, "I just stepped in poison ivy"!

    B Mom called "Don't forget to brush your teeth."

    C Nathan said that he was shopping for a new car.

    D "can anyone use some zucchini?" asked Jerome.

2. F The deliveryman asked? "where do you want the sofa"

    G Brandon advised "Don't quit your day job."

    H Caitlin shouted, Throw the ball to me!

    J "I wanted to see the sunrise," said Noah, "but I overslept."

3. A "Does anyone know how to program this VCR," asked Lisa?

    B "The forecaster said that tonight would be clear and cold."

    C Todd said, "The ceremony will begin at noon."

    D "The auctioneer cried," what will you give for this lovely quilt?

4. F Kelly asked, "Do you need some help in the kitchen?"

    G The princess complained, "that her bed was uncomfortable."

    H The waiter said, "today's special is meatloaf."

    J "It's almost quitting time." Brett said happily.

Read each sentence and look at the underlined part. Choose the answer that is written correctly for each underlined part.

5. The operator asked, "What number are you <u>calling</u>"

    A calling".

    B calling?"

    C calling"?

    D Correct as it is

6. "The butterfly," said the museum <u>guide, "Is</u> a fascinating creature."

    F guide "is

    G guide, is

    H guide, "is

    J Correct as it is

7. The chef <u>said that he</u> used only the freshest ingredients.

    A said, "That he

    B said that, he

    C said that, He

    D Correct as it is

8. Byron <u>remarked "This</u> play is hard to follow."

    F Byron remarked, "This

    G Byron remarked this

    H Byron remarked", This

    J Correct as it is

Using the Apostrophe: Contractions

Use an apostrophe (') when writing contractions. A **contraction** is a single word that combines two words. For example, instead of saying *does not*, you might substitute the contraction *doesn't*. When you write a contraction, insert an apostrophe in place of the one or more letters you have dropped from the words.

Some contractions are formed by combining a pronoun and a verb or helping verb, as in these examples:

he + is = he's	they + are = they're
she + is = she's	we + are = we're
it + is = it's	we + will = we'll
I + am = I'm	what + is = what's
I + have = I've	you + will = you'll

Often contractions are formed by combining a helping verb and the word *not*. The letters *o* or *no* are replaced by an apostrophe.

can + not = can't	have + not = haven't
could + not = couldn't	was + not = wasn't
did + not = didn't	were + not = weren't
do + not = don't	should + not = shouldn't
has + not = hasn't	would + not = wouldn't

This contraction is unusual: will + not = won't.

Choose the contraction that is formed by combining each pair of words. Write the contraction on the line.

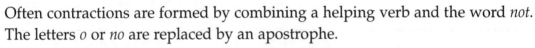

hasn't	can't	won't	I'll
shouldn't	it's	he's	they're

1. should + not = _____

2. has + not = _____

3. can + not = _____

4. I + will = _____

5. it + is = _____

6. he + is = _____

7. they + are = _____

8. will + not = _____

Practice

Rewrite each sentence using a contraction.

1. We will be at your house at eight o'clock sharp.

   _____

2. It has not been easy to concentrate lately.

   _____

3. If you are in the neighborhood, stop by.

   _____

4. I would not complain if I were you.

   _____

5. There are not any vacancies at this motel tonight.

   _____

6. I have forgotten where I parked my car again!

   _____

Read each of the following pairs of sentences. Choose the sentence in which the contraction is written correctly.

7. **A** The waiter shouldv'e brought us our meals ten minutes ago.

   B The waiter should've brought us our meals ten minutes ago.

8. **A** The express bus doesn't stop at Ashby Road.

   B The express bus does'nt stop at Ashby Road.

9. **A** If you're patient, you'll see the yellow finch at the bird feeder.

   B If you'er patient, youl'l see the yellow finch at the bird feeder.

10. **A** Theres' only one main road in my hometown.

    B There's only one main road in my hometown.

Apply

This passage contains eight contractions that have been formed incorrectly. Circle them. Then write them correctly, in order of appearance, on the numbered lines below.

Wel'l have our annual company picnic this Saturday, rain or shine. Weve planned a great day for you and your families. Among the activities scheduled are a baseball game and a water balloon toss. We're sure youll enjoy the delicious picnic lunch the boss has planned. Hel'l be flipping hamburgers all afternoon. Do'nt forget to bring your swimsuits. Two lifeguards have been hired. Theyll' be poolside all day. For evening fun, if youd like to stay late, there will be a campfire complete with scary stories and folk songs. This is our way of saying thanks. If it were'n't for all of you, this company wouldn't be doing as well as it has been this year. See you there!

1. _____   5. _____

2. _____   6. _____

3. _____   7. _____

4. _____   8. _____

Read the following paragraph. Underline any eight pairs of words that can be combined to form contractions. Then on the lines below, write the pairs of words and the contractions that could replace them. The first one is done for you.

If you are planning a trip this summer, please keep our resort in mind. We are not that far from your city, and we have a lot to offer you and your family. It should not be hard to picture yourself in one of our deluxe rooms. You will be pampered from morning to night. We will not rest until you are happy. Do not worry about finding someone to watch the kids, either. We have hired trained sitters who will see to it that your kids have as much fun as you have. You probably can not believe how reasonable our rates are. Do not wait too long. Our rooms are filling fast.

you + are = you're   ____ + ____ = _____

____ + ____ = _____   ____ + ____ = _____

____ + ____ = _____   ____ + ____ = _____

____ + ____ = _____   ____ + ____ = _____

Check Up

Read each group of sentences. Choose the sentence in which the contraction is written correctly.

1. **A** The painters hav'nt finished the job yet.

   B Its' supposed to be sunny and warm all week.

   C Did you know that I'm a certified scuba diver?

   D Whenever sh'es around, we're extra careful.

2. **F** You couldv'e been hurt badly.

   G There's a telephone call for Mr. Davis.

   H We didnt' know that the Hargroves still lived there.

   J The bakery clerk willn't wait on you unless you take a number.

3. **A** I couldn't complete today's crossword puzzle.

   B The workers were'nt happy with the company's offer.

   C When Tabitha drives, sh'es a menace on the highway.

   D Its getting late; let's go home.

4. **F** Wheres the principal's office?

   G Shouldn't' we be making dinner now?

   H Twenty minutes from now, you'll be Mrs. Wayne Franklin.

   J The airline cant find my brother's luggage.

Read each sentence and look at the underlined word. Choose the answer that is written correctly for the underlined word.

5. <u>Theyr'e</u> moving into a condo next month.

   A They'r'e

   B They're

   C Theyre'

   D Correct as it is

6. Erika <u>wasn't</u> happy about the extra work on Friday afternoon.

   F wasn't'

   G was'nt

   H wasnt

   J Correct as it is

7. <u>Id</u> be delighted to join you for dinner.

   A I'd

   B I'd'

   C Id'

   D Correct as it is

8. It seems that roller coasters <u>are'nt</u> as much fun as they used to be.

   F ar'ent

   G arent'

   H aren't

   J Correct as it is

Using the Apostrophe: Possessive Nouns

Use an apostrophe (') when writing possessive nouns. A **possessive noun** shows ownership or possession of the noun that follows it. Usually, only people or animals can possess.

> Rita's house   Bill's laugh

To make the possessive form of a noun, follow these rules.

- If the noun is singular, add an apostrophe and the letter s. Follow this rule even when the singular noun ends in s.

  Jackie's Deli   Charles's car

- If the noun is plural and ends in s, just add an apostrophe to the end of the word.

  the witches' brooms   the workers' cubicles

- If the noun is plural but does not end in s, add an apostrophe and an s.

  men's shoes   children's books

Circle the possessive noun in each sentence. On the line, write *S* for singular or *P* for plural.

1. _____ Melinda's fish tank needs cleaning.

2. _____ Often, ballet dancers' feet become bruised and painful.

3. _____ I could barely hear that actor's lines.

4. _____ For my parents' anniversary party, we have rented a tent.

5. _____ Roy Jones's dog won first prize at the dog show.

6. _____ The announcer called out one doctor's name after the other.

7. _____ The pianists' fingers flew through the duet.

8. _____ Please show me your line of women's bikes.

9. _____ The secretary brought the letter to Ms. Lopez's attention.

10. _____ The reports must be on the boss's desk tomorrow morning.

Practice

For each item, write a phrase that has the same meaning as the given phrase but uses a possessive noun.

       Example: the blankets that belong to the babies

                       the babies' blankets

1. the helmets that belong to the divers   _____

2. the cup that belongs to Tony   _____

3. the home that belongs to the Sadlers   _____

4. the handshake that Gloria has   _____

5. the ears of the elephant   _____

6. the laughter of the children   _____

7. the backpacks that belong to the hikers   _____

8. the tips that belong to the waitress   _____

Circle the possessive noun in each sentence. If it is not written properly, rewrite it correctly on the line. If it is written properly, write *Correct*.

9. Put the guests coats where they can find them easily.

_____

10. I knocked on the directors' door, and he invited me into his office.

_____

11. No two writers' penmanship is exactly the same.

_____

12. It has always been Bess' dream to own her own home.

_____

13. Two contestants in the mens' pole vault event were tied.

_____

14. The dentist's office was open, but he was out to lunch.

_____

Apply

In each sentence, find a phrase that can be changed to include a possessive noun. Then rewrite the sentence using that possessive noun.

1. The tools that belong to the gardener are stored in the shed.

   _____

2. The giggle of my daughter always makes me laugh.

   _____

3. Dave wrote the name of his brother on the emergency form.

   _____

4. The announcement could hardly be heard over the noise of the fans.

   _____

5. Sarah adjusted the brakes on the bike that belongs to her sister.

   _____

6. An aide picked up the suitcase that belongs to the governor.

   _____

7. This exam will test the basic skills of the students.

   _____

8. The speeches of the two candidates were similar.

   _____

9. The score that belongs to Marcus was the highest in the class.

   _____

10. Work was done on the locker room that belongs to the women.

    _____

Check Up

Read each group of sentences. Choose the sentence in which the possessive noun is written correctly.

1. **A** The farmers's hopes faded as the drought continued.

   B Her children were testing the young mother's patience.

   C We found an excellent picture book in the childrens' section.

   D The car was packed with the twin's' belongings.

2. **F** The bellboy took the travelers' suitcases up to their rooms.

   G Robertos' brother got a job in the factory.

   H The prisoner's families came to see them during visiting hours.

   J Cats curiosity sometimes gets them into trouble.

3. **A** Artis' workshop is filled with expensive tools.

   B The celebrity refused to answer the journalists questions.

   C The singer's throat was sore, so he went to the doctor.

   D The peoples' cheers made the hero feel welcome.

4. **F** Malik's' shopping cart had one wheel that wouldn't turn.

   G It's my hope to make my childrens dreams come true.

   H Tina couldn't take her eyes off the actress' sequined dress.

   J The chef's special included tacos and burritos.

Read each sentence and look at its underlined word. Choose the answer that is written correctly for each underlined word.

5. The winning <u>jockeys</u> outfit was splashed with mud.

   A jockey's

   B jockeys'

   C jockey's'

   D Correct as it is

6. Those <u>artists'</u> use of color is what sets them apart.

   F artists

   G artist's

   H artistss'

   J Correct as it is

7. It is the <u>voter's</u> right to expect honesty from their elected officials.

   A voter's'

   B voters'

   C voters

   D Correct as it is

8. <u>Megs'</u> hobbies include tennis and needlepoint.

   F Meg's'

   G Meg's

   H Megs

   J Correct as it is

Writing Friendly Letters

Use a friendly, informal letter when you want to keep in touch with friends and family members. A typical friendly letter has five parts. The letter below shows how and where to write each part.

The **heading** is the date when you write the letter. Insert a comma between the day of the month and the year. A friendly, informal letter does not need an inside address.

The **salutation**, also called the **greeting**, begins with the word *Dear*, is capitalized, and in an informal letter ends with a comma. Every word in the name is capitalized.

The **body** is your message, the main part of the letter.

The body is followed by the **closing**. Only the first word of the closing is capitalized. The closing ends with a comma. Last comes your **signature**. In an informal letter, you don't need to print or type your name below your signature.

(Heading)	January 12, 2005
(Salutation)	Dear Sue,
(Body)	Did you have a good New Year's? We went to a fireworks celebration downtown. It was a little cold, but everybody had a great time. What did you do for New Year's?
(Closing)	Best wishes,
(Signature)	*Donna*

Identify each part of a friendly letter below. If it contains errors, rewrite it correctly on the second line.

1. April 12 2005 _____ _____

2. With Love, _____ _____

3. Dear Mary ann _____ _____

4. *Luis Valadez* _____ _____

Practice

The following parts of a letter are out of order. Some of the parts have capitalization or punctuation errors. Using the friendly letter format shown on the previous page as a placement guide, write each part correctly in its proper place on the letter form below.

Dear Sasha: june 22, 2005

Sincerely Yours   *Roger*

    How are you? I'm wondering what your plans are for the rest of the summer. I'd love to have you come for a visit if you can get away for a few days. Let me know what your schedule looks like.

_____

_____

_____

_____

_____

_____

_____

_____

_____

_____

Apply

Now practice writing a real letter to a friend or relative. Start with today's date. In the salutation, put the name of the person you're writing to. Write a paragraph or two about what's going on in your life: your job, your home life, your classes, whatever you want to tell this person. Then write a paragraph about the person the letter is to. You might ask how he or she is and recount a favorite memory you share. Be sure to capitalize and punctuate the letter correctly.

_____

_____

_____

_____

_____

_____

_____

_____

_____

_____

_____

_____

Check Up

Read the following letter and look at its underlined parts. Choose the answer that is written correctly for each underlined part.

(1)   august 10, 2005

(2)   Dear Nathaniel:

(3)   I just got back from a long swim, and it made me think of you. Are you still training as hard as you did when we worked out together. I've slowed down a bit, but I still enjoy swimming.

(4)   I don't think I've seen you since I switched jobs. I'm working for a much smaller company now. I'm still doing data entry which is not the most exciting work in the world. But I like the people, and the atmosphere is cozy.

(5)   I hope all is well with you. I have to take the dog for a walk now, so I'll drop this in the mail while I'm out.

(6)   Best Wishes

        Pavel

1. **A** august 10 2005
    B August 10 2005
    C August 10, 2005
    D Correct as it is

2. **F** Dear Nathaniel
    G Dear Nathaniel,
    H dear Nathaniel,
    J Correct as it is

3. **A** together, I've
    B together? I've
    C together I've
    D Correct as it is

4. **F** data entry, which is
    G data, entry which is
    H data entry which, is
    J Correct as it is

5. **A** now. So I'll
    B now, so I'll
    C now? So I'll
    D Correct as it is

6. **F** Best wishes
    G Best Wishes,
    H Best wishes,
    J Correct as it is

Writing Business Letters

Use a business letter when you need to communicate formally. A business letter has seven parts. The letter below shows how and where to write each part.

The **heading** is the date on which the letter is written. Insert a comma between the day of the month and the year.

The **inside address** is the recipient's address. It usually has three lines: the name of the individual or business; the street address or post office box; and the city, state, and zip code. Capitalize all proper nouns in the inside address. If the address includes a post office box, capitalize *P.O.* Remember to insert a comma between the names of the city and the state. Use the common two-letter, capitalized abbreviation for the state.

The **salutation**, also called the **greeting**, begins with the word *Dear*, is capitalized, and always ends with a colon. Capitalize *Sir* and *Madame* if you don't know the name.

The **body** is the writer's message. It is followed by the **closing.** Only the first word of the closing is capitalized. The closing ends with a comma. Last comes the writer's **signature** followed by his or her **name**, printed clearly below the signature.

(Heading)	September 24, 2005
(Inside Address)	Abandoned No More
	4638 Oak Street
	Berkeley, CA 94710
(Salutation)	Dear Mr. Blake:
(Body)	Please accept my donation to your fund for abandoned animals.
(Closing)	Sincerely yours,
(Signature)	*Hillary Brown*
(Name)	Hillary Brown

Identify each letter part below. If it contains errors, rewrite it correctly on the line.

1. Yours Truly,   _____ _____

2. june, 3 2004   _____ _____

3. p.o. Box 145   _____ _____

Practice

The following parts of a letter are out of order. Some of the letter parts have capitalization or punctuation errors. Using the letter format shown on the previous page as a placement guide, write each letter part correctly in its proper place on the letter form below.

Wacky Websites company

Yours Truly;

Everett Thomas

Houston TX, 77573

Everett Thomas

1719 Enterprise Parkway

may, 29, 2005

Dear Human resources director,

I recently earned a certificate in Web design and am seeking a job in the computer field. In addition to knowing how to make Web sites, I am familiar with many software programs. Please consider me for the job advertised in the newspaper last Sunday.

_____

_____

_____

_____

_____

_____

_____

_____

_____

_____

_____

_____

_____

_____

Apply

Use the following information to write a business letter on the lines below. Give the letter today's date. Write a letter to Traver Photography at 3621 Bedford Street in Tomahawk, Wisconsin. The zip code is 54487. Tell Ms. Traver that you wish to buy more photographs of your son, whose picture was taken at school by Traver Photography. You would like to find out the prices for various sizes of photos. Be sure to capitalize and punctuate the letter correctly.

_____

_____

_____

_____

_____

_____

_____

_____

_____

_____

_____

_____

_____

_____

_____

Check Up

Read the following letter and look at its underlined parts. Choose the answer that is written correctly for each underlined part.

(1) <u>March 19 2004</u>

Dearborn Camera

(2) <u>2745 Main Street</u>

(3) <u>alexandria va, 22314</u>

(4) <u>dear Mrs. Greyton:</u>

    I have been thinking of buying a digital camera. I hope to use the photographs

(5) in a <u>newsletter so I</u> need high quality equipment. Please send me information about your cameras, along with complete descriptions and a price list.

(6) <u>sincerely yours:</u>

Emily Farrell

Emily Farrell

1. **A** march 19, 2004

   B March, 19 2004

   C March 19, 2004

   D Correct as it is

2. **F** 2745 main street

   G 2745, Main Street

   H 2745 Main street

   J Correct as it is

3. **A** alexandria, VA 22314

   B Alexandria, VA 22314

   C Alexandria VA 22314

   D Correct as it is

4. **F** dear Mrs. Greyton,

   G Dear Mrs. Greyton:

   H Dear Mrs. Greyton,

   J Correct as it is

5 **A** newsletter, so I

   B newsletter. So I

   C newsletter; so i

   D Correct as it is

6. **F** Sincerely yours,

   G Sincerely Yours,

   H Sincerely Yours:

   J Correct as it is

Review

Writing Quotations

Direct quotations present a speaker's exact words in quotation marks.

"Would you like a cup of coffee?" Darlene asked. "This pot will be ready soon."

"That would be nice," Anna said.

An **indirect quotation** does not use the speaker's exact words or quotation marks

Darlene asked Anna if she wanted a cup of coffee.

Writing Contractions

A **contraction** combines two words. An apostrophe replaces one or more letters.

I + am = I'm   was + not = wasn't

Writing Possessive Nouns

A **possessive noun** shows ownership of the noun that follows it.

Singular: Add apostrophe and *s*. (the chef's specialty)

Plural ending in *s*:   Add apostrophe. (the girls' scarves)

Plural not ending in *s*:   Add apostrophe and *s*. (women's club)

Writing a Letter

A business letter has seven parts. A friendly, informal letter has five of those parts.

(Heading)   February 8, 2005

(Inside Address)   Euclid Electronics

(business letter only)   1294 Appian Way

                            Greensburg, PA 15650

(Salutation)   Dear Customer Service Manager:

(end with comma
in friendly letter)

(Body)   Please send your latest catalog to the address on
                            this letterhead. Thank you.

(Closing)   Best regards,

(Signature)   *Jeffrey Chodra*

(Name)   Jeffrey Chodra

(printed name not needed
in friendly letter)

Assessment

Read each group of sentences. Choose the sentence that is written correctly.

1. **A** "Our garden needs weeding," said Mrs. Carlton.

   B Ned asked, "How many calories are there in a cup of buttermilk"

   C Tricia suggested, "Let's go to the new pizza place tonight"!

   D The singer announced, "this will be our last song."

2. **F** "This time" warned the sheriff, "You'd better tell the truth."

   G "In my opinion," said Linda, "you've had enough brownies."

   H "the fact is," explained Bob "you've overstayed your welcome."

   J "When I give you a nod" said Eric, "we'll leave."

3. **A** The fundraiser announced, that the goal had been reached.

   B "Don't forget to endorse your check," advised Sam.

   C Carla exclaimed "We put in a bid on the house"!

   D "The conductor said, Show me your ticket."

4. **F** If you ca'nt drive any faster, we'll miss the plane.

   G Youl'l be the first to know if I get the job.

   H I wouldn't want you to go to any trouble for me.

   J The scouts are tent camping tonight, so theyl'l be cold.

5. **A** The wardrobe manager outdid herself on that actress' costume.

   B "Where are that young mans manners?" said Grandma.

   C The receptionists' voice was clear and friendly.

   D The museum will display both artists' work this month.

6. **F** Tracys presentation was brief but interesting.

   G The teacher pushed all the student's desk's into the hall.

   H The coach ordered new uniforms for the mens' basketball team.

   J When the Russells went away, I took care of Molly's cat.

7. **A** As Mike ran after the bus, he shouted "Stop"!

   B Alice complains, "That she never feels rested anymore."

   C "Who sent me this beautiful bouquet?" asked Vicky.

   D "I know it's late" said Jim, "But I can't leave yet."

8. **F** I'm telling you that you won't even know the difference.

   G Were still going to have the cookout even if it rains.

   H Who has'n't dreamed of winning a million dollars?

   J Rose said she'd bring baked bean's to the picnic.

Read the following letters and paragraph and look at their underlined parts. Choose the answer that is written correctly for each underlined part.

(9)   November, 4 2005

Value Grocery Store

(10)   4591 Barracks boulevard

(11)   Boulder, CO 80302

(12)   Dear Mr. Wright:

(13)   Our local club, the Womens' Guild of Boulder, is raising money to supply food to needy families this winter. We are hoping you can help us. Would you consider sending us a small donation or some non-perishable foods to distribute? Thank you in advance.

(14)   Gratefully yours

Nell Jones

Nell Jones

9. **A** November 4, 2005

    B november 4, 2005

    C November 4 2005

    D Correct as it is

10. **F** 4591 Barracks boulevard,

    G 4591 Barracks Boulevard

    H 4591 barracks boulevard

    J Correct as it is

11. **A** Boulder, co, 80302

    B boulder co 80302

    C boulder CO, 80302

    D Correct as it is

12. **F** Dear Mr. Wright,

    G Dear Mr. Wright:

    H dear Mr. Wright:

    J Correct as it is

13. **A** Womens's' Guild of Boulder

    B Women's' Guild Of Boulder

    C Women's Guild of Boulder

    D Correct as it is

14. **F** Gratefully yours;

    G Gratefully Yours,

    H Gratefully yours,

    J Correct as it is

(15) November 1, 2005

(16) dear Luisa,

     Thank you so much for the birthday present. The necklace is the perfect color for me. I wore it to dinner Saturday night and got **(17)** lots of compliments. Your such a thoughtful friend.

(18) Sincerely Yours,
      Armenita

15. A November 1 2005

    B november 1, 2005

    C November, 1, 2005

    D Correct as it is

16. F dear Luisa:

    G Dear Luisa:

    H Dear Luisa,

    J Correct as it is

17. A compliments, your

    B compliments. You're

    C compliments; your

    D Correct as it is

18. F Sincerely Yours:

    G Sincerely yours

    H Sincerely yours,

    J Correct as it is

(19)   Have you ever heard of phrenology? Its a practice based on the belief that different parts of the brain control different parts of one's personality. **(20)** Phrenologists believed that they could identify peoples' strongest personality traits by feeling the bumps on their heads. Unfortunately believers couldn't prove that this method really worked. We now know that each individual's personality cannot be understood in such a simple way.

19. A Its's

    B I'ts

    C It's

    D Correct as it is

20. F people's

    G people's'

    H peoples

    J Correct as it is

Posttest

Decide which punctuation mark, if any, is needed in each sentence.

1. "When is the meeting scheduled to begin? asked Lorraine.

    A ' **B** . **C** " **D** None

2. Bring the following items to the workshop scissors, paste, and construction paper.

    F " **G** : **H** , **J** None

3. Look out below

    A ? **B** ! **C** . **D** None

4. "When Mr. Lambert arrives" said the mayor, "show him into my office."

    F " **G** , **H** ; **J** None

5. Nikki can you give me a hand with this box?

    A , **B** : **C** . **D** None

Choose the word or phrase that best completes each sentence.

6. Irene and I _____ the entire house tomorrow.

    F vacuum

    G vacuumed

    H will vacuum

    J have vacuumed

7. Jake needs a new car, but _____ can't afford it now.

    A he

    B they

    C you

    D it

8. Mary Ann _____ in the park every morning before she began working the night shift.

    F have walked

    G walks

    H walk

    J had walked

9. Last summer the environmental club _____ up the riverbank.

    A clean

    B cleaned

    C will clean

    D cleans

Choose the sentence in each set that is written correctly and has correct capitalization and punctuation. Be sure the sentence you choose is complete.

10. **F** A perfect day for baseball.

    G The umpire near first base who was signaling the runner.

    H Ran out onto the field.

    J The coach signaled to the batter.

11. **A** Dana likes the Mall on center Street.

    B Don't you love to sit quietly in a japanese Garden?

    C Is the garbage collection on Thursday or on Friday this week?

    D My Doctor gave me a Shot.

12. **F** The bus company is rising the fares again next month.

    G Grandma is learning Courtney how to quilt.

    H The train schedule is lying on the counter.

    J Lay down for a few minutes.

13. **A** The children were tired, they had been busy all day.

    B The audience is restless; the band is an hour late.

    C Every night at the same time.

    D The sun has set it's getting cold.

14. **F** The garage sale was a success.

    G "how can I help?" Brian asked.

    H Sara writes for the *Springfield observer.*

    J Stephen Foster wrote the old song "beautiful Dreamer."

15. **A** "Do you think you'll be finished on time" asked the customer.

    B "The cabinets," said the contractor, "Are on the way."

    C "I'll be glad when this project is done." said Adam.

    D Faith cried, "How beautiful my new kitchen looks!"

16. **F** I'm not sure theyr'e coming.

    G Didnt we send them invitations?

    H Do you have the host's' address?

    J Len will park all the guests' cars.

17. **A** I don't have no idea what he said.

    B Tony won't never come back.

    C The pilot could hardly see through the dense fog.

    D There wasn't nothing anyone could do to improve the situation.

18. **F** Try more harder next time.

    G I chose the slowest checkout line.

    H Of all the photos of my vacation, I like this one better.

    J Please speak more slowlier.

19. **A** My cold was terrible, but it didn't last long.

    B Can you find the light switch, and turn the lights on?

    C The day was; hot Rob went jogging anyway.

    D Some people take chances but, others like to play it safe.

Read each set of underlined sentences. Then choose the sentence that best combines those sentences.

20. Sleep sofas are on sale today.
    Easy chairs are on sale today.

    F Sleep sofas and easy chairs are on sale today.

    G Today, sleep sofas are on sale and so are easy chairs on sale.

    H On sale today are sleep sofas, and easy chairs are on sale today, too.

    J Sleep sofas with easy chairs are on sale today.

21. Kali waved to the bus driver.
    Kali waved frantically.
    He didn't see her.

    A Frantically, the bus driver didn't see Kali even though she was waving.

    B Kali waved to the bus driver frantically, and he didn't see her waving.

    C Kari waved frantically to the bus driver, but he didn't see her.

    D Waving to the bus driver frantically, he didn't see Kali.

22. Francine wore a new dress to the party.
    The dress was black.

    F Wearing a new black dress, Francine went to the party.

    G At the party, Francine wore a dress that was both new and black.

    H Francine wore a new black dress to the party.

    J The dress that Francine wore to the party was new, and it was black.

23. Many people paid for the concert tickets with cash.
    Other people paid for the concert tickets with credit cards.

    A At the concert, many people paid for tickets using cash and credit cards.

    B Many people paid for the concert tickets with cash, and others paid with credit cards.

    C Cash was the way some people paid for the concert tickets, but credit cards were the way other people paid for the concert tickets.

    D Even though many people like to pay cash for things like concert tickets, it sometimes happens that other people pay for concert tickets using credit cards.

Read each paragraph. Then choose the sentence that best fills the blank.

24.   Michael follows the same routine every morning. After getting up and getting dressed for work, he picks up the newspaper from the front step. _____. While the coffee is being made, he reads the front page. When the coffee is ready, he pours himself a cup, picks up the paper, and runs for the bus.

  F   Next he puts sugar and cream in his coffee.

  G   Next he puts on a pot of coffee.

  H   Next he opens the front door.

  J   Next he decides what to wear to work that day.

25.   Gene and Olivia went to their favorite restaurant. _____. While they waited for the pizza to come, they talked about what had happened to them that day. When the pizza finally came, they dove in with enthusiasm.

  A   They paid their check and left.

  B   They couldn't decide what to order when the server came to their table.

  C   They asked for more napkins because the pizza was messy.

  D   They ordered a pizza with mushrooms and onions.

26.   _____. They washed and waxed all the hardwood floors in the main rooms. They dusted and vacuumed the bedrooms. They washed the windows, and they even cleaned the attic and the basement.

  F   The house was large, with five bedrooms and large living and dining rooms.

  G   Spring cleaning is an annual tradition in our household.

  H   The cleaners we hired did a thorough house cleaning.

  J   The house looked so much better after it was clean.

27.   _____. Perhaps a big grandfather clock would enhance your home's decor. Maybe your tastes run to a simple school clock, with its clean face and easily visible numbers. You may just need an alarm clock for your bedroom or a decorative clock to set on your mantel.

  A   There is bound to be a clock to match your needs.

  B   Grandfather clocks must be wound every week, or they will run down.

  C   The alarm on my clock is annoying, but it works well.

  D   Not many local stores have a good selection of clocks.

Read each topic sentence. Then choose the answer that best develops the topic sentence.

28. Natasha spent all day in the old barn.

   F A barn-raising is an event for the entire community. Everyone does his or her part.

   G She married Paul ten years ago. They have two daughters and a son.

   H The air was cool and smelled of sweet hay. Sunlight filtered in through cracks between the boards.

   J She has short dark hair, with a little gray at the temples. Her eyes are light brown.

29. Preserving historic buildings should be a national priority.

   A Old buildings are a link to our past. Preserving them will allow us to enjoy the beauty of these places now and in the future.

   B Many old buildings have been allowed to deteriorate badly. Some may even be dangerous and should be torn down.

   C Buildings constructed long ago do not conform to modern building requirements. Almost none of them have good plumbing or heating systems.

   D Should old buildings be outfitted with air conditioning? Or would installing air conditioning make the buildings less historic?

30. William Shakespeare's plays are still popular.

   F William Shakespeare was a playwright who was born in England in 1564. He did most of his work in London, England.

   G Shakespeare wrote both tragedies and comedies. One of his most famous plays is *Romeo and Juliet.*

   H In Shakespeare's days, women were not allowed to be actors. For that reason, the female roles were originally played by men.

   J Every year, high schools all over the country put on Shakespeare's plays. Annual drama festivals usually feature one or more of his works, and the festivals are always well attended.

Read each paragraph. Then choose the sentence that does <u>not</u> belong in the paragraph.

31.   **1.** The Thanksgiving Day parade is a favorite among local clubs and organizations. **2.** Troops from the Girl Scouts and Boys Scouts always march in it. **3.** City government always sends some representatives, especially those who plan to run for office soon. **4.** To see the parade best, stand on Main Street near the library.

A Sentence 1

B Sentence 2

C Sentence 3

D Sentence 4

32.   **1.** San Marino, just east of Florence, Italy, is one of the smallest countries in the world. **2.** It has a population of only 4,179. **3.** Italy has attracted tourists for centuries. **4.** San Marino's total area is a tiny 24 square miles.

F Sentence 1

G Sentence 2

H Sentence 3

J Sentence 4

33.   **1.** Martin has been having trouble with his computer lately. **2.** Computer prices have been going down steadily. **3.** When Martin turns the computer on, it is taking longer and longer for the opening screen to appear. **4.** Every now and then, for no obvious reason, the computer screen freezes.

A Sentence 1

B Sentence 2

C Sentence 3

D Sentence 4

34.   **1.** At work, we dress in casual clothes on Friday. **2.** Maintaining a business-like appearance is essential for many jobs. **3.** Receptionists must look neat and attractive. **4.** Professional people must dress in a way that inspires confidence.

F Sentence 1

G Sentence 2

H Sentence 3

J Sentence 4

Read the following paragraphs and letter and look at their numbered, underlined parts. Choose the answer that is written correctly for each underlined part.

(35)   Listening to the radio October 30, 1938, <u>a panic swept America.</u> An urgent voice over the radio reported that aliens from Mars had landed
(36) in New Jersey. Listeners <u>didnt'</u> realize that the story was fictional.
(37) Frightened people bombarded the radio station with <u>phone calls, some</u> jumped into their cars and tried to escape. When the play was done, people were relieved but also angry to discover that the broadcasters
(38) <u>had fooled them.</u> *The War of the Worlds* had just been too real for comfort.

35. **A** Americans panicked

      B a panicky feeling was felt

      C the announcer made Americans panic

      D Correct as it is

36. **F** did'nt

      G didn't

      H did'n't

      J Correct as it is

37. **A** phone calls some

      B phone calls. Some

      C phone calls. some

      D Correct as it is

38. **F** fool them

      G fools them

      H has fooled them

      J Correct as it is

(39)   This year's film festival includes the following classic <u>movies:</u> *Gone with the Wind* and *The Maltese Falcon*. The response to our
(40) request for suggestions <u>were</u> overwhelming. At our next meeting,
(41) <u>Senator alfonzo Lopez</u> will share a list of his favorite political
(42) thrillers. The meeting promises to be the <u>most interestingly</u> of the season. See you there!

39. **A** movies;

      B movies

      C movies,

      D Correct as it is

40. **F** was

      G have been

      H are

      J Correct as it is

41. **A** senator Alfonzo Lopez

      B Senator alfonzo lopez

      C Senator Alfonzo Lopez

      D Correct as it is

42. **F** more interestingly

      G most interesting

      H interestingest

      J Correct as it is

(43) June 13, 2003

Barnes Consulting Service
(44) p.o. box 472
(45) Portland or 97205

(46) Dear Ms. allen;
(47)   I am writing in response to your ad in the *portland register*. I understand that you are planning to expand your department. My
(48) resume is attached. Please keep I in mind for any available position.

        Sincerely yours,

        Sam Lewis

        Sam Lewis

43. **A** June 13; 2003

    B June, 13, 2003

    C june 13 2003

    D Correct as it is

44. **F** P.o. Box 472

    G P.O. Box 472

    H P.O. box: 472

    J Correct as it is

45. **A** Portland OR 97205

    B Portland OR, 97205

    C Portland, OR 97205

    D Correct as it is

46. **F** Dear Ms. Allen:

    G dear Ms. Allen;

    H dear Ms. Allen:

    J Correct as it is

47. **A** *Portland register*

    B *portland Register*

    C *Portland Register*

    D Correct as it is

48. **F** mine

    G me

    H my

    J Correct as it is

Read the following friendly letter. Notice the numbered, underlined parts. Choose the answer that is written correctly for each underlined part.

(49)　　　august 29, 2005

(50)　　Dear Mom:

(51)　　　　I just wanted to let you know that I'm getting settled in my dorm room? You were right, it was a good idea to come to school a few days before classes started. It gave me time to learn my way around campus and meet some people.

　　　　Speaking of people, I'm afraid my new roommate is as unusual as our first impressions suggested. She wears black nail polish and listens to punk rock.
(52)　　Looking at her, she's stuck in the 1980s. Still, she's getting more friendly, and she offered to lend me her laptop, so I'll see how it goes.

(53)　　　　Well, I raised with the sun today for orientation, so I have to get to bed. I'll talk to you over the weekend.

(54)　　　　With much Love,

　　　　Chandra

49. **A** august 29 2005

　　B august 29: 2005

　　C August 29, 2005

　　D Correct as it is

50. **F** Dear Mom

　　G Dear Mom,

　　H dear Mom

　　J Correct as it is

51. **A** room.

　　B room:

　　C room!

　　D Correct as it is

52. **F** When I look at her, I think

　　G Looking at her

　　H When I look at her,

　　J Correct as it is

53. **A** I rose

　　B I was rising

　　C me raised

　　D Correct as it is

54. **F** With Much Love,

　　G With much love,

　　H With much Love

　　J Correct as it is

Read each paragraph. Then choose the sentence that best fills the blank.

55.   In Kevin's yard, the main color of spring is yellow. The very first thing to flower, sometimes when there's still snow on the ground, is coltsfoot. Its flowers are as bright as dandelions. Then come the forsythia shrubs that line his driveway. _____. The yard is yellow for at least a month before it starts to look green.

 A After that, daffodils and tulips bloom.

 B However, daffodils and tulips bloom.

 C As a result, daffodils and tulips bloom.

 D For instance, daffodils and tulips bloom.

56.   Humans appeared at least two million years ago. Early on, they began making tools. Then they learned to use fire, which let them cook food. Eventually they created language. _____. When they developed agriculture, they were able to stay in one place and grow food.

 F At first, their tools were getting more sophisticated.

 G For many thousands of years, humans foraged over large areas for food.

 H They also learned to communicate by symbols.

 J The first modern humans appeared in Africa.

Read the following paragraphs and look at their numbered, underlined parts. Choose the answer that is written correctly for each underlined part.

(57)   There are more than 9,000 species of birds. Nearly all of <u>they</u> can fly. For
(58) example, eagles and hawks soar thousands of feet above the ground. <u>They soars</u>
(59) on <u>thermals,</u> or currents of warm air. From such heights they can spot a mouse on
(60) the ground. They're so graceful that <u>he's</u> beautiful to watch.

57. **A** their

    B thems

    C them

    D Correct as it is

58. **F** They soar

    G Them soar

    H They is soaring

    J Correct as it is

59. **A** thermals or

    B thermals or,

    C thermals; or

    D Correct as it is

60. **F** he's;

    G their

    H they're

    J Correct as it is

(61)   George Sanchez, <u>my neighbor</u> is on a diet. When he wasn't looking, he
(62) gained thirty pounds. He tried a high-protein diet, but when <u>he laid</u> down at
      bedtime, he could feel his heart pounding. Now he's eating lots of fruits and
(63) vegetables. The <u>Sanchezes'</u> are all supporting his effort. His children have quit
(64) eating junk food. His <u>wife, marta,</u> works out with him every day.

61. **A** my, neighbor,

    B my neighbor,

    C my Neighbor

    D Correct as it is

62. **F** he lay

    G he layed

    H him laid

    J Correct as it is

63. **A** Sanchez's

    B Sanchezes

    C Sanchez'

    D Correct as it is

64. **F** wife marta

    G Wife, Marta,

    H wife, Marta,

    J Correct as it is

Posttest Answer Key and Evaluation Chart

This Posttest has been designed to check your mastery of the language skills studied. Circle the question numbers that you answered incorrectly and review the practice pages covering those skills.

Key

1.	C	31.	D
2.	G	32.	H
3.	B	33.	B
4.	G	34.	F
5.	A	35.	A
6.	H	36.	G
7.	A	37.	B
8.	J	38.	J
9.	B	39.	D
10.	J	40.	F
11.	C	41.	C
12.	H	42.	G
13.	B	43.	D
14.	F	44.	G
15.	D	45.	C
16.	J	46.	F
17.	C	47.	C
18.	G	48.	G
19.	A	49.	C
20.	F	50.	G
21.	C	51.	A
22.	H	52.	F
23.	B	53.	A
24.	G	54.	G
25.	D	55.	A
26.	H	56.	G
27.	A	57.	C
28.	H	58.	F
29.	A	59.	D
30.	J	60.	H
		61.	B
		62.	F
		63.	B
		64.	H

Tested Skills	Question Numbers	Practice Pages
pronouns	48, 60	25–28, 29–32
antecedent agreement	7, 57	33–36
verbs	6, 9, 38	37–40, 41–44, 45–48
subject/verb agreement	8, 40, 58	49–52
easily confused verbs	12, 53, 62	53–56
adjectives and adverbs	18, 42	57–60, 61–64, 65–68
use of negatives	17	69–72
sentence recognition	10, 13, 37	77–80, 81–84
sentence combining	20, 21, 22, 23	85–88, 89–92
sentence clarity	35, 52	93–96, 97–100
topic sentences	26, 27	105–108, 109–112
supporting sentences	28, 29, 30	113–116, 117–120
sequence	24, 25	121–124
unrelated sentences	31, 32, 33, 34	125–128
transitions, connective words	55, 56	129–132
proper nouns and proper adjectives	11, 41	137–140, 141–144
first words and titles	14, 47	145–148
end marks	3, 51	153–156
commas	5, 19, 59, 61, 64	157–160, 161–164, 165–168, 169–172, 173–176
semicolons and colons	2, 39	177–180
quotations	1, 4, 15	185–188
apostrophes	16, 36, 63	189–192, 193–196
business letter parts	43, 44, 45, 46	201–204
friendly letter parts	49, 50, 54	197–200

Answer Key

Unit 1 Usage

Nouns
Page 21
1. company, manager, salary,
2. Ernesto, accident, road, **3.** trip, Texas, Nick, Austin, San Antonio, **4.** Jenny, dress, dinner, restaurant, **5.** flowers, wind,
6. Middle Ages, time, knights, castles,
7. waiter, diners, courtesy, tip, **8.** Katie, time, Depot Street, map, **9.** March, Smiths, Palm Beach, Florida, **10.** Miners, California, gold

Page 22
1. *Underline:* world, Charles Goodyear, material, rubber; *Circle:* People,
2. *Underline:* rubber, Goodyear, substance,
3. *Underline:* rubber; *Circle:* days,
4. *Underline:* rubber; *Circle:* days,
5. *Underline:* Goodyear, substance,
6. *Underline:* inventor, discovery; *Circle:* years, experiments, **7.** *Underline:* Rubber, chemical, sulfur, **8.** *Underline:* Goodyear, discovery; *Circle:* debts, rights, **9.** *Underline:* inventor; *Circle:* people, **10.** *Underline:* Charles Goodyear, contribution; *Circle:* moments, **11.** The citizens of New York were thrilled when the Brooklyn Bridge opened. **12.** After Lauren moved into her apartment, she sewed new window curtains. **13.** Correct, **14.** The Atlas Mountains are located in Africa.
15. Eleanor Roosevelt worked for the welfare of all Americans. **16.** Steven and his family came from Barbados, an island in the Caribbean Sea. **17.** Correct

Page 23
Answers will vary.

Page 24
1. C, **2.** F, **3.** B, **4.** J, **5.** B, **6.** F, **7.** D, **8.** H, **9.** A, **10.** J

Personal Pronouns
Page 25
1. *Underline:* her; *Arrow to:* Fiona,
2. *Underline:* they; *Arrow to:* players,
3. *Underline:* you; *Arrow to:* Grandmother; *Underline:* he; *Arrow to:* Dad, **4.** *Underline:* her, she; *Arrows to:* Dana, **5.** *Underline:* I; *Arrow to:* Marvin, **6.** *Underline:* he; *Arrow to:* author,
7. *Underline:* its; *Arrow to:* bird

Page 26
1. us, **2.** He, **3.** her, **4.** they, **5.** I,
6. him, **7.** me, **8.** we, **9.** him, **10.** She,
11. them, **12.** her, **13.** I, **14.** They, **15.** us

Page 27
1. *Underline:* its; *Circle:* car,
2. *Underline:* his; *Circle:* Kyle, **3.** *Underline:* theirs; *Circle:* Wildcats, **4.** *Underline:* my; *Circle:* I, **5.** *Underline:* hers; *Circle:* Ilene,
6–10: Answers will vary. Possible answers are given. **6.** my, your, his, her, **7.** mine, yours, ours, his, hers, theirs, **8.** My, Your, Our, His, Her, Their, **9.** my, our, your, his, her, their, **10.** mine, ours, his, hers, theirs

Page 28: 1. B, **2.** H, **3.** D, **4.** H, **5.** D, **6.** G, **7.** A, **8.** H, **9.** D, **10.** G

Other Kinds of Pronouns
Page 29
1. *Underline:* that; *Arrow to:* computers,
2. *Underline:* who; *Arrow to:* driver,
3. *Underline:* himself; *Arrow to:* doctor,
4. *Underline:* that; *Arrow to:* symphony,
5. *Underline:* whose; *Arrow to:* man,
6. *Underline:* itself; *Arrow to:* dog, **7.** *Underline:* whom; *Arrow to:* suspect, **8.** *Underline:* herself; *Arrow to:* Maria, **9.** *Underline:* that; *Arrow to:* car, **10.** *Underline:* myself; *Arrow to:* I

Answer Key continued

Page 30

1. themselves, **2.** themselves,
3. herself, **4.** himself, **5.** herself, **6.** herself,
7. himself, **8.** yourself, **9.** myself,
10. yourself, **11.** that; REL, **12.** that; REL,
13. himself; REF, **14.** herself; REF,
15. that; REL, **16.** themselves; REF,
17. that; REL, **18.** who; REL, **19.** who;
REL, **20.** whom; REL

Page 31

1. himself, **2.** itself, **3.** herself, **4.** who,
5. Who, **6.** themselves, **7.** herself, **8.** who,
9. ourselves, **10.** whom, **11–16:** Sentences
will vary. The required pronoun must be
used correctly in each sentence.

Page 32

1. B, **2.** F, **3.** B, **4.** J, **5.** B, **6.** F, **7.** C, **8.** H

Making Pronouns Agree with Their Antecedents

Page 33

1. diners, P, **2.** pandas, P, **3.** landscaper, S,
4. oatmeal, S, **5.** jacket, N, **6.** Dan, M,
7. Karen, F, **8.** book, N

Page 34

1. Hector, 3, **2.** I, 1, **3.** protesters, 3, **4.** You,
2, **5.** peaches, 3, **6.** *Underline:* he; *Circle:*
Sean, **7.** *Underline:* whose; *Circle:*
homeowner, **8.** *Underline:* their; *Circle:*
astronauts, **9.** *Underline:* themselves;
Circle: Kelly, Celeste, **10.** *Underline:* its;
Circle: bear, **11.** *Underline:* her; *Circle:*
Laura, **12.** *Underline:* which; *Circle:* home,
13. *Underline:* myself; *Circle:* I,
14. *Underline:* them; *Circle:* bagels

Page 35

1. After Mike got his paycheck, he deposited
<u>it</u> in the bank. **2.** Correct, **3.** The cows slowly
lifted <u>their</u> heads when the farmer
approached. **4.** The king and <u>his</u> court
enjoyed the juggler's act. **5.** The prize should
go to the dancer <u>who</u> wore the red costume.
6. Correct, **7.** Grandmother is proud of <u>her</u>
grandchildren. **8.** Mia drove slowly because
<u>she</u> could barely see through the fog.
9. Please give me the files so I can study
<u>them</u>. **10.** Fans begged the actress for <u>her</u>
autograph.

Page 36

1. B, **2.** F, **3.** C, **4.** G, **5.** A, **6.** J,
7. A, **8.** H

Verbs

Page 37

1. lost, **2.** were, **3.** struck, **4.** leaves, must
buy, **5.** reads, is, **6.** was, **7.** attend, are, is,
8. stumbled, **9.** was repaired, **10.** fell,
covered

Page 38

1. R, **2.** IR, **3.** R, **4.** IR, **5.** IR, **6.** IR, **7.** IR,
8. IR, **9.** R, **10.** IR, **11.** R, **12.** R, *From the
paragraph:* burned, thought, tried, cut,
forgotten, left, broke, meant, changed,
said, looked, served

Page 39

1. *Underline:* sponsored; action,
2. *Underline:* travel; action, **3.** *Underline:* is;
linking, **4.** *Underline:* sold; action,
5. *Underline:* has ruined; action,
6. *Underline:* guarded; action, **7.** *Underline:*
are; linking, **8.** C, **9.** H, **10.** B, **11.** F, **12.** C,
13. F

Page 40

1. B, **2.** F, **3.** A, **4.** H, **5.** B, **6.** J, **7.** D, **8.** G

Answer Key continued

Simple Tenses of Verbs

Page 41
1. *Underline:* will pay, Future,
2. *Underline:* disagrees, Present,
3. *Underline:* picked, Past, 4. *Underline:* fixes, breaks; Present, 5. *Underline:* will stop, Future, 6. *Underline:* had, delivered; Past, 7. *Underline:* looks, Present,
8. *Underline:* moved, Past; *Underline:* is, Present

Page 42
1. A, 2. A, 3. B, 4. B, 5. A, 6. B, 7. A, 8. B, 9. A, 10. B

Page 43
1. A sang, B will sing, 2. A saw, B see,
3. A will fight, B fought, 4. A will spill,
B spilled, 5. A reads or will read,
B read, 6. will explain, 7. traveled,
8. wants, 9. will return, 10. will experience

Page 44
1. A, 2. F, 3. B, 4. G, 5. C, 6. F, 7. C, 8. J

Perfect Tenses of Verbs

Page 45
1. *Underline:* changed, runs, had complained; *Write:* had complained,
2. *Underline:* has collected, will have donated; *Write:* has collected, will have donated, 3. *Underline:* has offered, will fit; *Write:* has offered, 4. *Underline:* had hired, received; *Write:* had hired, 5. *Underline:* have exchanged, met; *Write:* have exchanged, 6. *Underline:* will sell, will have put; *Write:* will have put

Page 46
1. A Present, B Past, C Future, 2. F Past, G Present, H Future, 3. A Future, B Past, C Past, 4. had washed, 5. has sung, 6. have received, 7. will have bought, 8. will have finished

Page 47
1. A, 2. B, 3. A, 4. A, 5. had planned,
6. had grabbed, 7. will have completed,
8. has stood, 9. will have cleared, 10. will have used

Page 48
1. A, 2. H, 3. D, 4. J, 5. C, 6. J, 7. B, 8. J

Agreement of Subjects and Verbs

Page 49
1. Correct, 2. go, 3. is, 4. Correct, 5. Correct,
6. am, 7. try, 8. prunes, 9. sit, 10. Correct

Page 50
1. *Underline:* book, script; *Circle:* and; *Underline:* are; *Write:* P, 2. *Underline:* chain, stores; *Circle:* or; *Underline:* carry; *Write:* P, 3. *Underline:* lamps, fixture; *Circle:* nor; *Underline:* gives; *Write:* S, 4. *Underline:* pennies, dime; *Circle:* and; *Underline:* make; *Write:* P, 5. *Underline:* sisters, Mr. Van Ness; *Circle:* or; *Underline:* has; *Write:* S, 6. is,
7. are, 8. shows, 9. sit, 10. watch, 11. calls,
12. slide

Page 51
1. problem is, 2. Prices have,
3. Children were, 4. Photographs capture,
5. one was, 6. questions trick, 7. Dorothy has

Page 52
1. C, 2. G, 3. D, 4. F, 5. D, 6. G, 7. A, 8. H

Easily Confused Verbs

Page 53
1. lay, 2. rise, 3. teach, 4. raise, 5. lie,
6. learn

Page 54
1. A, 2. A, 3. B, 4. A, 5. B, 6. B, 7. Lie,
8. teach, 9. rises, 10. lay, 11. raised,
12. Raise, 13. lay, 14. laid, 15. learned

Answer Key continued

Page 55

1. My sister taught me how to ride a bike when I was five. 2. We lay in our sleeping bags and looked up at the stars.
3. The landlord says he will raise the rent next month. 4. Correct, 5. We saw the sun rise beside some pink clouds. 6. Correct,
7. Correct, 8. We should lay the new area rug in the guest bedroom. 9. The custodian raises the flag every morning. 10. Correct, 11. The wedding dress had lain in the old chest for years. 12. Correct

Page 56

1. A, 2. G, 3. C, 4. J, 5. C, 6. F, 7. B, 8. H

Adjectives

Page 57

1. small, brown, 2. third, early, 3. local, empty, rusty, 4. new, brighter, old, 5. home, gray,
6. important, 7. nearby, discount, cheapest,
8. kind, flat, 9. highest, 10. wet, muddy

Page 58

1. sunnier, 2. best, 3. saddest, 4. more or less peaceful, 5. wiser, 6. most or least perfect,
7. deepest, 8. drier, 9. Correct, 10. worse,
11. Correct, 12. most loyal, 13. prettiest,
14. better

Page 59

Answers will vary.

Page 60

1. B, 2. J, 3. A, 4. H, 5. C, 6. J, 7. C, 8. F

Adverbs

Page 61

1. noisily, 2. now, 3. never,
4. more loudly, 5. boldly, 6. quickly,
7. most clearly, 8. recently, 9. Yes, 10. less vigorously, 11. almost, 12. carefully

Page 62

1. roughly, 2. most roughly, 3. sooner,
4. soonest, 5. badly, 6. worst, 7. neatly,
8. more neatly, 9. earlier, 10. earliest,
11. most sweetly, 12. Correct, 13. safely,
14. better, 15. more quietly, 16. Correct,
17. farthest, 18. Correct

Page 63

1–4. Answers will vary. 5. B, 6. B, 7. A,
8. A, 9. A, 10. A

Page 64

1. B, 2. J, 3. A, 4. G, 5. C, 6. J, 7. C, 8. F

Adjective or Adverb?

Page 65

1. ADJ, 2. ADV, 3. ADV, 4. ADV, 5. ADV,
6. ADV, 7. ADV, 8. ADV, 9. ADJ,
10. ADV, 11. ADJ, 12. ADJ

Page 66: 1. *Underline:* sweeter; *Circle:* taste,
2. *Underline:* angrily; *Circle:* glared,
3. *Underline:* good; *Circle:* recipe, 4. *Underline:* widest; *Circle:* paintbrush, 5. *Underline:* most beautiful; *Circle:* one, 6. *Underline:* badly;
Circle: plays, 7. *Underline:* more clever; *Circle:* You, 8. *Underline:* warmer; *Circle:* water,
9. *Underline:* smoothest; *Circle:* fudge,
10. *Underline:* continuously; *Circle:* barked,
11. *Underline:* nearly; *Circle:* fell,
12. *Underline:* most silently; *Circle:* moves

Page 67

1. A wettest, B wetly, C wetter, 2. F firmly,
G firmest, H more firmly, 3. A more restful,
B more restfully, C restful, 4. F most daringly, G more daring, H daring.
5–9. Answers will vary, but the form must match the form listed here. 5. comparative form of adjective, 6. adverb, 7. superlative form of adverb, 8. adverb, 9. superlative form of adjective

Page 68
1. A, 2. H, 3. C, 4. J, 5. B, 6. G, 7. D, 8. H

Using Negative Words Correctly
Page 69
1. doesn't, no, 2. don't, hardly, 3. Correct, 4. Didn't, no one, 5. Correct, 6. haven't, nothing, 7. Doesn't, nobody, 8. don't, nowhere, 9. can't, hardly, 10. didn't, none

Page 70
1. ever, 2. was, 3. anything, 4. any, 5. anywhere, 6. any, 7. anyone, 8. anything, 9. any, 10. were, 11. B, 12. F, 13. C, 14. H, 15. A

Page 71
Answers will vary. Possible answers are provided. 1. Moira's car won't ever start on cold mornings. *or* Moira's car will never start on cold mornings. 2. I hardly had time to relax before I had to cook dinner. *or* I didn't have time to relax before I had to cook dinner. 3. I don't want any of you to worry about me. *or* I want none of you to worry about me. 4. Correct, 5. My cat doesn't jump onto the furniture anymore. 6. Erika didn't want anything to spoil her perfect evening. *or* Erika wanted nothing to spoil her perfect evening. 7. Don't let anyone in while I am away. *or* Let no one in while I am away. 8. Nancy never wants any mushrooms on her pizza. *or* Nancy wants no mushrooms on her pizza ever. 9. Correct, 10. Lamar never has any time to watch TV anymore. *or* Lamar has no time to watch TV anymore.

Page 72
1. C, 2. F, 3. C, 4. J, 5. B, 6. H, 7. D, 8. F

Assessment
Pages 73–76
1. A, 2. J, 3. D, 4. H, 5. A, 6. H, 7. B, 8. G, 9. C, 10. J, 11. A, 12. H, 13. C, 14. G, 15. C, 16. G, 17. D, 18. G, 19. B, 20. H, 21. A, 22. H, 23. A, 24. H, 25. C, 26. J

Unit 2 Sentence Formation

Complete Sentences and Fragments
Page 77
1. F, 2. F, 3. CS (*Underline:* Leonard; *Circle:* didn't buy the motorcycle), 4. F, 5. CS (*Underline:* The painting; *Circle:* is in a gold frame), 6. F, 7. F, 8. F, 9. CS (*Underline:* Harry; *Circle:* mowed the lawn yesterday), 10. CS (*Underline:* Lucia's apartment, *Circle:* is on the fifth floor)

Page 78
1. CS, 2. Clause, 3. Clause, 4. Phrase, 5. CS, 6. Phrase, 7. Clause, 8. CS, 9. CS, 10. Phrase

Page 79
Answers will vary.

Page 80
1. B, 2. F, 3. B, 4. J, 5. B, 6. H

Answer Key continued

Run-On Sentences

Page 81

1. The Cotton Club is downtown,/they have live music on Saturdays. 2. We went to the beach/the kids love to swim. 3. Don cleaned out the cupboard,/he found his army knife in there. 4. Scott broke the VCR,/he's trying to fix it himself. 5. Warren is a great cook/his wife is lucky. 6. Ellen went home/she lives in Chicago. 7. They're charging three dollars for a soda,/I don't think I'm thirsty. 8. She plays softball,/he runs five miles a day. 9. CS, 10. RO, 11. CS, 12. RO, 13. RO, 14. RO

Page 82

1. B, 2. B, 3. A, 4. B, 5. A

Page 83

Answers will vary for numbers 2, 3, 5, 6, 9, and 10. Possible answers are given. 1. CS, 2. Dana has to leave work early; she has a dental appointment. 3. The Ferris wheel is fun, but I like the roller coaster better. 4. CS, 5. Teresa had to go home and change. Her shirt was stained with motor oil. 6. Victor knew that the pasta was overcooked; nevertheless, he took a giant helping. 7. CS, 8. CS, 9. The newspaper costs fifty cents. Can I borrow a dime? 10. These shoes are too tight; they're giving me blisters.

Page 84

1. B, 2. H, 3. A, 4. G, 5. B, 6. H

Sentence Combining: Compound Sentence Parts

Page 85

1. *Underline:* scares my dog; *Write:* Thunder and lightning scare my dog. 2. *Underline:* Jian; *Write:* Jian plays violin and tutors music students. 3. *Underline:* witnessed the accident; *Write:* Mr. Silva and his son witnessed the accident. 4. *Underline:* are loaded with calories; *Write:* Ice cream sundaes and chocolate cakes are loaded with calories. 5. *Underline:* The band; *Write:* The band performed its hit songs and thrilled the audience. 6. *Underline:* Alex; *Write:* Alex jacked up the car and changed the flat tire.

Page 86

1. *Underline:* The actor has starred in; A, 2. *Underline:* The magazine article is; B, 3. *Underline:* Carla pays her bills early; B, 4. *Underline:* Ms. Kerr praised the; B, 5. *Underline:* We bought fresh, at the Farmers' Market; A

Page 87

1. Will you please pass the salt and pepper? 2. Correct, 3. Bears and ground squirrels hibernate in the winter. 4. Paul and Liz baked some delicious cookies. 5. Kristen filed the receipts and orders for the week. 6. The security guard at the airport inspected the suitcases and backpacks.

Page 88

1. B, 2. H, 3. D, 4. J

Answer Key continued

Sentence Combining: Adding Modifiers
Page 89
1. (car) Ralph's old car stopped in the middle of the street. 2. (masks) As a hobby, the Greenes collect masks from Africa. 3. (bonus) The manager gave a small bonus to each worker.
4. (ring) That opal ring in the jewelry case is beautiful. 5. (cottage) Leslie rented a summer cottage near the lake.

Page 90
1. D, 2. C, 3. E, 4. B, 5. A, 6. F

Page 91
1. The trainer spoke firmly and calmly to the restless horse. 2. Miriam purchased an elegant gown for her wedding. 3. Correct, 4. A singer entertained the crowd from ten until midnight. 5. Correct

Page 92
1. B, 2. H, 3. D, 4. H, 5. A, 6. H

Sentence Clarity: Misplaced Modifiers
Page 93
1. You can see a heron standing in the pond. 2. The children who live next door brought mail addressed to me. 3. Correct, 4. Janet joined the health club in her office building for more exercise. 5. All the vegetables lying on the lower shelf in the refrigerator are from our garden.
6. Correct

Page 94
1. B, 2. A, 3. B, 4. A, 5. B, 6. B, 7. A, 8. B

Page 95
1. A, 2. H, 3. B, 4. G, 5. C

Page 96
1. D, 2. G, 3. A, 4. H, 5. C, 6. J

Sentence Clarity: Parallel Structure
Page 97
1. B, 2. A, 3. B, 4. B, 5. A, 6. B

Page 98
1. C, 2. F, 3. B, 4. J, 5. C, 6. G

Page 99
1. C, 2. G, 3. B, 4. G, 5. D, 6. F

Page 100
1. D, 2. F, 3. B, 4. H, 5. C, 6. G, 7. D, 8. G

Assessment
Pages 102–104
1. B, 2. J, 3. A, 4. G, 5. B, 6. H, 7. D, 8. J, 9. C, 10. F, 11. C, 12. G, 13. D

Unit 3 Paragraph Development

The Main Idea of a Paragraph
Page 105
1. B; *Underline:* Charles got great news from the palm reader. 2. G; *Underline:* Pickled foods can be found in all parts of the world.

Page 106
1. E, 2. A, 3. B, 4. D, 5. C

Page 107
Answers will vary. Possible answers are given. 1. There is always something new at the art museum. 2. Chutneys are a versatile addition to any meal. 3. It is important to organize your work area well. 4. Spanish missionaries thought that California was an ideal location for their work.

Page 108
1. D, 2. G, 3. D, 4. H, 5. A

Answer Key continued

Finding the Topic Sentence

Page 109

1. The ancient Greeks believed that different gods controlled different parts of the weather. **2.** All of the contestants had imaginative hairstyles. **3.** Good habits can help you study better.

Page 110

1. C, **2.** G, **3.** C, **4.** F

Page 111

Answers will vary. Possible answers are given. **1.** You can take evening classes in just about any subject. **2.** Monkeys come in many sizes. **3.** Portland, Oregon, is a sports-loving city. **4.** My friend Jake is what some people call a "neat freak."

Page 112

1. C, **2.** H, **3.** B, **4.** F

Developing Paragraphs with Details and Examples

Page 113

1. Examples; *Topic sentence:* Dublin, Ireland, was home to many famous writers. **2.** Sensory Details; *Topic sentence:* Visiting my grandmother's house is like going back in time.

Page 114

1. examples, A, **2.** sensory details, G, **3.** examples, C

Page 115

Answers will vary.

Page 116

1. D, **2.** F, **3.** C

Developing Paragraphs with Reasons, Facts, and Figures

Page 117

1. Topic Sentence, **2.** Supporting Sentence

Page 118

1. Reasons, **2.** Facts and Figures, **3.** Facts and Figures, **4.** Reasons, **5.** Reasons

Page 119

1. reasons, B, **2.** facts and figures, F, **3.** facts and figures, C, **4.** reasons, G

Page 120

1. D, **2.** H, **3.** A, **4.** F

Recognizing the Order of Events

Page 121

1. C, **2.** G

Page 122

1. 2, 3, 1, 4, **2.** 1, 4, 2, 3, **3.** 4, 3, 2, 1, **4.** 3, 4, 1, 2, **5.** 3, 2, 1, 4

Page 123

1. B, C, A, D, **2.** F, H, J, G, **3.** B, D, A, C, **4.** G, J, F, H

Page 124

1. B, **2.** H, **3.** D

Answer Key continued

Identifying an Unrelated Sentence
Page 12
1. C, 2. G

Page 126
Wording of answers will vary. Possible answers are given. 1. *Main idea:* how maple syrup is made; *Cross out:* One of America's favorite breakfasts is pancakes. *Reason:* The connection between pancakes and maple syrup is not made clear.
2. *Main idea:* why Holly's favorite month is September; *Cross out:* Holly roots for the Pleasanton Pheasants. *Reason:* Knowing the football team that Holly roots for does not help to explain why she likes September. 3. *Main idea:* the clothes Melisa buys at secondhand stores; *Cross out:* He had been a World War II general. *Reason:* Eishenhower's career is not relevant to Melisa's taste in clothing. 4. *Main idea:* why some people believe that baseball is a dying sport in America; *Cross out:* In Europe, soccer is called football. *Reason:* The paragraph is about baseball in America, not soccer in Europe.

Page 127
1. *Cross out:* Many city dwellers see rats in their neighborhoods even today. 2. *Cross out:* State colleges are usually cheaper than private ones. 3. *Cross out:* You can see an active volcano in Hawaii. 4. Correct, 5. *Cross out:* Philadelphia is a historic city in Pennsylvania.

Page 128
1. C, 2. J, 3. C, 4. G

Transition and Connective Words
Page 129
1. *Underline:* So; cause and effect;
2. *Underline:* Immediately; time;
3. *Underline:* Similarly; compare

Page 130
1. D, 2. A, 3. C, 4. E, 5. B

Page 131
1. First, 2. However, 3. Finally, 4. On the other hand, 5. Inside, 6. For example, 7. Finally, 8. The next day, 9. Because of

Page 132
1. D, 2. G, 3. A

Assessment
Pages 134–136
1. C, 2. J, 3. B, 4. H, 5. D, 6. G, 7. C, 8. H, 9. D, 10. G 11. C

Unit 4 Capitalization

Capitalizing Proper Nouns and *I*
Page 137
1. Cousin Michael, 2. I, Uncle Charles, 3. Judge Kim, Senator Blake, 4. Mary Ann Evans, George Eliot, 5. Mrs. Linda J. Helm, 6. Governor Mike A. Thompson, 7. Aunt Carla, Dr. Saunders, 8. Coach Davis, I, 9. Superintendent Barbara Dade, 10. Prof. Lewis

Page 138
1. B, 2. B, 3. A, 4. B, 5. A, 6. Correct, 7. Senator Jennifer Spencer, 8. Timothy A. Hamilton, 9. Uncle Fred, 10. Professor Butler, 11. Mr. Eugene H. Clark, 12. Correct, 13. Dr. Steven J. Garofalo, 14. Alex T. Dixon, 15. W. C. Fields

Page 139

1. We hired Mr. Jeff Reynolds to take pictures at the wedding. **2.** The street was named for General Robert E. Lee. **3.** My grandfather and Uncle Louis love to go fishing. **4.** Your tour guide will be Ms. Diana Carr. **5.** My father and I met Mr. Blair in Dr. Chin's office. **6.** We are having a dinner in honor of Coach Lopez. **7.** Have you seen the old photos taken by Grandpa Brady? **8.** She and Erica have applied for the job of security guard. **9.** Both Mayor G. W. Lang and Councilman Bill Weld were reelected. **10.** My friends and I listened to some old records by Jimi Hendrix.

Page 140

1. D, **2.** H, **3.** A, **4.** F, **5.** B, **6.** J, **7.** C, **8.** G

Capitalizing Proper Nouns and Proper Adjectives

Page 141

1. Field Museum, Natural History, Chicago, **2.** Belgian, Canadian, **3.** Spanish, Wednesday, **4.** Aleutian Islands, Alaska, **5.** Springtown Library, Bluebell Street, **6.** New York City, Thanksgiving, **7.** Blair Building, First Street, **8.** Claremont Juggling Club, **9.** Paris, France, American Airlines

Page 142

1. Memorial Day, **2.** Seattle, Washington, **3.** the month of May, **4.** Chrysler Building, **5.** National Geographic Society, **6.** Lake Erie, **7.** southern New Mexico, **8.** Correct, **9.** Rodeo Drive, **10.** Correct, **11.** B, **12.** B, **13.** B, **14.** A, **15.** A

Page 143

1. We saw Mount Rushmore in South Dakota last summer. **2.** I bought a chair at Jordan's Furniture Store. **3.** We drove across the Peace Bridge over the Niagara River. **4.** This store sells bikes made by the Prentiss Company. **5.** Have you seen the Chinese paintings at the Cleveland Museum of Art? **6.** The French ship sailed through the Panama Canal. **7.** Meet me at the corner of Market Street and Powell Street. **8.** The city of Houston, Texas, is about fifty miles from the Gulf of Mexico. **9.** I start working at Mervyn's Department Store on Saturday. **10.** The Mojave Desert is in southern California.

Page 144

1. B, **2.** H, **3.** A, **4.** G, **5.** B, **6.** H, **7.** A, **8.** J

Capitalizing First Words and Titles

Page 145

1. The, A.M., **2.** Everyone, The Stars, Stripes Forever, **3.** One, *The Maltese Falcon*, **4.** The, These, **5.** One, *The New York Times*, **6.** Send, P.O. Box, **7.** When, **8.** My, *Nightmare, Elm Street*, **9.** The, Do, **10.** *The Twilight Zone*

Page 146

1. *The Sound of Music*, **2.** *Life on the Mississippi*, **3.** "The King of Cotton Candy", **4.** *The Wall Street Journal*, **5.** *Candid Camera*, **6.** Correct, **7.** "The Open Boat", **8.** Correct, **9.** B, **10.** A, **11.** A, **12.** B, **13.** B, **14.** B, **15.** A

Answer Key continued

Page 147
1. "Enjoy your meal," said the waiter.
2. This recipe is from *Family Circle*. **3.** My alarm clock rings at 6:45 A.M. **4.** Did you read the article in *The Washington Post*?
5. Mail your request to P.O. Box 10.
6. "Our first game will be tomorrow," said the coach. **7.** The clerk asked, "Can I help you?" **8.** My sister's favorite book is *The Old Man and the Sea*. **9.** The salesman assured me, "This is a great car." **10.** The poem "Elegy for Jane" is quite sad.

Page 148
1. A, **2.** J, **3.** D, **4.** G, **5.** A, **6.** G, **7.** C, **8.** J

Assessment
Pages 150–152
1. B, **2.** J, **3.** C, **4.** F, **5.** D, **6.** G, **7.** B, **8.** J, **9.** C, **10.** H, **11.** A, **12.** G, **13.** C, **14.** F, **15.** B, **16.** F, **17.** D, **18.** H, **19.** C, **20.** G, **21.** B, **22.** H, **23.** A, **24.** J

Unit 5 Punctuation

End Marks
Page 153
1. . **2.** ? **3.** . . **4.** ! **5.** . . **6.** ! **7.** ! **8.** ? **9.** !

Page 154
1. A, **2.** B, **3.** A, **4.** A, **5.** A, **6.** B, **7.** B, **8.** F, **9.** D, **10.** H, **11.** A, **12.** G

Page 155
Sentences will vary. They should relate to the given situations and end with the proper end marks.

Page 156
1. B, **2.** G, **3.** D, **4.** J, **5.** A, **6.** F, **7.** B, **8.** H, **9.** A, **10.** H, **11.** A

Commas in Compound Sentences
Page 157
1. not circled, **2.** circled; comma after *dishes*, **3.** circled; comma after *museum*, **4.** not circled, **5.** circled; comma after *attention*, **6.** not circled, **7.** circled; comma after *good*, **8.** not circled, **9.** circled; comma after *sight*, **10.** circled; comma after *usual*

Page 158
1. A **2.** B, **3.** B, **4.** A, **5.** A, **6.** insert comma after *loads*, **7.** no comma needed, **8.** insert comma after *walk*, **9.** insert comma after *longer*, **10.** no comma needed, **11.** insert comma after *difficult*, **12.** insert comma after *vegetarian*, **13.** insert comma after *today*, **14.** insert comma after *trail*, **15.** no comma needed

Page 159
1. insert comma after *features*, **2.** *X* over comma, **3.** *X* over comma, **4.** C, **5.** insert comma after *now*, **6.** insert comma after *rare*, **7.** C, **8.** insert comma after *station*, **9.** *X* over comma, **10.** insert comma after *now*, **11.** C, **12.** *X* over comma, **13.** insert comma after *fear*, **14.** *X* over comma, **15.** C, **16.** B, **17.** A, **18.** A

Page 160
1. A, **2.** J, **3.** C, **4.** G, **5.** B, **6.** F, **7.** D, **8.** H

Commas in Complex Sentences
Page 161
1. insert comma after *night*,
2. insert comma after *fits*, **3.** no comma,
4. insert comma after *anything*, **5.** no comma, **6.** insert comma after *made*, **7.** no comma, **8.** insert comma after *useless*,
9. insert comma after *o'clock*, **10.** no comma,
11. insert comma after *hill*, **12.** no comma

Answer Key continued

Page 162

1. B, **2.** A, **3.** A, **4.** B, **5.** A, **6.** insert comma after *harder*, **7.** no comma, **8.** insert comma after *sunrise*, **9.** insert comma after *November*, **10.** no comma, **11.** insert comma after *test*, **12.** no comma, **13.** insert comma after *landed*, **14.** insert comma after *intermission*, **15.** insert comma after *alarm*, **16.** insert comma after *hides*

Page 163

1. X over comma, **2.** X over comma, **3.** insert comma after *complicated*, **4.** X over comma after *step*, **5.** X over comma, **6.** C, **7.** insert comma after *class*, **8.** C, **9.** C, **10.** C, **11.** insert comma after *soon*, **12.** insert comma after *clients*, **13.** insert comma after *client*, **14.** X over comma, **15.** C, **16.** A, **17.** B, **18.** A

Page 164

1. A, **2.** F, **3.** C, **4.** G, **5.** C, **6.** J, **7.** A, **8.** H

Commas in Series

Page 165

1. guppies, goldfish, and tiger barbs, **2.** shook, shuddered, and collapsed, **3.** piles of magazines, stacks of books, and mounds of papers, **4.** Mr. Berg, Ms. Allen, or Dr. Pike, **5.** Correct, **6.** hot, tangy, and satisfying, **7.** mowed the lawn, trimmed the bushes, and watered the flowers, **8.** Correct, **9.** the dentist, her assistant, and the hygienist, **10.** swayed, clapped, or danced

Page 166

1. B, **2.** A, **3.** B, **4.** B, **5.** A, **6.** insert commas after *pages, copies,* **7.** insert commas after *angry, sullen,* **8.** insert commas after *soup, dessert,* **9.** insert commas after *Horses, sheep,* **10.** insert commas after *dishes, silverware,* **11.** C, **12.** insert commas after *foot, horseback,* **13.** insert commas after *Maurice, Jack,* **14.** insert commas after *museum, monuments,* **15.** insert commas after *barrels, signs*

Page 167

1. It was a hot, hazy, sultry day. **2.** Jerry, Laurie, Don, and Phyllis went to the air show. **3.** Clap your hands, stamp your feet, and twirl your partner. **4.** Rabbits, gray squirrels, and deer made their homes in the forest. **5.** Correct, **6.** Seagulls circled, swooped low, and gently landed on the water. **7.** Buy tuna steaks, fresh shrimp, or whitefish fillets for dinner. **8.** The tour bus stops at Hoover Dam, the Grand Canyon, and Four Corners. **9.** Will a birdbath, a trellis, or a bench look best in the garden? **10.** Correct

Page 168

1. D, **2.** H, **3.** A, **4.** G, **5.** A, **6.** G, **7.** D, **8.** F

Answer Key continued

Commas with Appositives

Page 169

1. <u>the playwright</u> explains *William Shakespeare*. 2. <u>an Englishwoman</u> explains *Aphra Behn*. 3. <u>the Steelers</u> explains *team*. 4. <u>or Saki</u> explains *H. H. Munro*. 5. <u>my favorite flowers</u> explains *hyacinths*.

Answers will vary. Sample answers:
1. Fran and Chloe, the Salinger twins, are in my class. 2. Ignatz Smith, the electrician, rewired my living room. 3. Bill Jones, the supervisor, gave Renee an excellent performance review. 4. Pauli and Dennis, my neighbors, went to Ireland last summer. 5. Tony O'Brien, a top student, wrote a very interesting term paper.

Page 170

1. Underline *a two-story Colonial* and set it off with commas before and after.
2. Underline *a member of the Cree tribe* and set it off with commas. 3. Underline *an old video game* and set it off with commas.
4. Underline *the oldest amusement park in the area* and set it off with commas.
5. Underline *or tree of heaven* and set it off with commas. 6. no appositive,
7. Underline *the empress of the blues* and set it off with commas. 8. Underline *the prince of Wales* and set it off with commas. 9. no appositive, 10. Underline *the fastest land animal in the world* and set it off with commas. 11. Insert commas after *stone* and *rock*. 12. no commas 13. Insert commas after *physics* and *subject*. 14. Insert commas after *21* and *solstice*. 15. no commas 16. Insert commas after *Aaron* and *batter*. 17. Insert commas after *subway* and *transport*. 18. Insert commas after *Rudbeckia* and *Susan*. 19. Insert commas after *Jordan* and *forward*.

Page 171

1. Danielle's husband, Roberto, often travels to Argentina. 2. Sam's only daughter, Elayne, graduated from the University of Pittsburgh. 3. Wolfgang is very good at playing his favorite instrument, the flute. 4. The red maple tree, also known as *acer rubrum*, has very colorful leaves in the fall. 5. no commas, 6. Eliza Habra, the mayor of Mt. Pleasant, plans to run for state senator. 7. Chickpeas, also known as garbanzo beans, are nutritious. 8. Ahmed Akbar, an antiques dealer, is an expert in illuminated manuscripts. 9. Olympic swimmer, Amanda Beard, won several medals in 2004. 10. Simone de Beauvoir, a leading existentialist, was born in 1908.

Page 172

1. A, 2. J, 3. D, 4. H, 5. A, 6. H, 7. C, 8. J

Other Uses of Commas

Page 173

1. A, 2. B, 3. B, 4. A, 5. A

Page 174

1. son, 2. Mike, 3. Dr. Blackburn, 4. sweetheart, 5. Sandy, 6. insert comma after *Thomas*, 7. insert comma after *Tucson*, 8. insert commas after *No, newspaper*, 9. insert commas after *tomorrow, Omaha*, 10. insert commas after *theater, gentlemen*, 11. insert comma after *day*, 12. insert commas after *Japan, Honolulu*, 13. insert comma after *air*, 14. insert commas after *Yes, Pamela*

Answer Key continued

Page 175

1. Yes, the tour bus stops in New Orleans, Louisiana. **2.** According to the map, we should have gotten off at the last exit, Stan. **3.** In time, William will understand. **4.** No, Nick, this is not the CD you wanted. **5.** If you need fuel, Dolly, stop at the next service station. **6.** Glittering in the sun, the spiderweb was breathtaking. **7.** Shortly after graduating from college, Beth moved to Denver, Colorado. **8.** Without the remote control, Kurt, nobody can change channels. **9.** At dawn they began the long trek to Arches National Park near Moab, Utah. **10.** Weak from exhaustion, Greta stepped across the finish line.

Page 176

1. C, **2.** F, **3.** A, **4.** H, **5.** D, **6.** F, **7.** B, **8.** G

Semicolons and Colons

Page 177

1. insert semicolon after *spring,* **2.** insert semicolon after *simple,* **3.** insert semicolon after *blue,* **4.** insert semicolon after *night,* **5.** insert semicolon after *Edith,* **6.** insert semicolon after *crowded,* **7.** insert semicolon after *weeks,* **8.** insert semicolon after *together,* **9.** insert semicolon after *burgers,* **10.** insert semicolon after *paper,* **11.** insert semicolon after *old,* **12.** insert semicolon after *desk,* **13.** insert semicolon after *buildings,* **14.** insert semicolon after *journal*

Page 178

1. A, **2.** A, **3.** A, **4.** B, **5.** insert semicolon after *sandwiches,* **6.** place *X* over colon, **7.** insert semicolon after *model,* **8.** insert colon after *ingredients*

Page 179

1. David sent out more than fifty applications; he finally got a good job. **2.** The audience rose and applauded wildly; the singers returned many times for bows. **3.** The storeroom has pens, paper, and staples; it has no notebooks. **4.** Success requires three things: skill, patience, and persistence. **5.** Heather sorted glass and plastic from cardboard and paper; she thinks that it is important to recycle. **6.** Our baby boy was born at 3:12 A.M. on Tuesday. **7.** The mailman came at 10:30; he delivered three catalogs. **8.** I never expected to win; I almost didn't enter the contest. **9.** The tour will visit these cities: Rome, Paris, and London. **10.** Diane works well with the people in her office; she hopes to become manager.

Page 180

1. A, **2.** H, **3.** C, **4.** F, **5.** B, **6.** J, **7.** A, **8.** H

Assessment

Pages 182–184

1. C, **2.** J, **3.** A, **4.** F, **5.** A, **6.** J, **7.** C, **8.** H, **9.** D, **10.** G, **11.** C, **12.** F, **13.** B, **14.** G, **15.** A, **16.** G, **17.** D, **18.** J, **19.** A, **20.** H, **21.** B, **22.** G, **23.** B, **24.** H, **25.** D

Unit 6 Writing Conventions

Writing Quotations
Page 185
1. The usher mumbled, "Go to the theater on the left." 2. IQ, 3. "Where is the petite department?" Karla asked the clerk. 4. IQ, 5. "Let's leave now!" whispered Leeann. 6. Vince asked, "Which late-night show is your favorite?" 7. The frightened woman cried, "My house is on fire!" 8. IQ, 9. IQ, 10. "Run for home!" Matt shouted. 11. IQ, 12. Jordan said, "I am finally getting used to decaf coffee."

Page 186
1. B, 2. B, 3. A, 4. A, 5. A, 6. B

Page 187
1. The librarian said, "Please be quiet in the library." 2. "I can proofread your letter," offered Ruth. 3. "My baby sleeps all day," complained Teresa, "and is awake all night." 4. no commas needed, 5. The night watchman shouted, "Stay where you are!" 6. "Our goal," said the director, "is to please every customer." 7. Marla asked, "Would you like a second helping?" 8. Correct, 9. "My computer crashed again!" whined Bobbi. 10. Gabe said, "I like strawberries in my cereal." 11. "This summer is hot," admitted Jon, "but last summer was hotter." 12. "Our team," complained the coach, "is getting too many penalties." 13. Aaron asked, "Have you heard any good jokes lately?" 14. "I run two miles every morning," said Michelle.

Page 188
1. C, 2. J, 3. C, 4. F, 5. B, 6. H, 7. D, 8. F

Using the Apostrophe: Writing Contractions
Page 189
1. shouldn't, 2. hasn't, 3. can't, 4. I'll, 5. it's, 6. he's, 7. they're, 8. won't

Page 190
1. We'll be at your house at eight o'clock sharp. 2. It hasn't been easy to concentrate lately. 3. If you're in the neighborhood, stop by. 4. I wouldn't complain if I were you. 5. There aren't any vacancies at this motel tonight. 6. I've forgotten where I parked my car again! 7. B, 8. A, 9. A, 10. B

Page 191
1. We'll, 2. We've, 3. you'll, 4. He'll, 5. Don't, 6. They'll, 7. you'd, 8. weren't, **Possible contractions for the second paragraph:** *Underline:* We are, *Write:* We're; *Underline:* we have, *Write:* we've; *Underline:* should not, *Write:* shouldn't; *Underline:* You will, *Write:* You'll; *Underline:* We will, *Write:* We'll; *Underline:* will not, *Write:* won't; *Underline:* you are, *Write:* you're; *Underline:* Do not, *Write:* Don't; *Underline:* We have, *Write:* We've; *Underline:* who will, *Write:* who'll; *Underline:* can not, *Write:* can't; *Underline:* Do not, Write: Don't

Page 192
1. C, 2. G, 3. A, 4. H, 5. B, 6. J, 7. A, 8. H

Using the Apostrophe: Writing Possessive Nouns
Page 193
1. Melinda's, S, 2. dancers', P, 3. actor's, S, 4. parents', P, 5. Roy Jones's, S, 6. doctor's, S, 7. pianists', P, 8. women's, P, 9. Ms. Lopez's, S, 10. boss's, S

Page 194

1. the divers' helmets, 2. Tony's cup, 3. the Sadlers' home, 4. Gloria's handshake, 5. the elephant's ears, 6. the children's laughter, 7. the hikers' backpacks, 8. the waitress's tips, 9. *Circle:* guests; *Write:* guests', 10. *Circle:* directors'; *Write:* director's, 11. *Circle:* writers'; *Write:* Correct, 12. *Circle:* Bess'; *Write:* Bess's, 13. *Circle:* mens'; *Write:* men's, 14. *Circle:* dentist's; *Write:* Correct

Page 195

1. The gardener's tools are stored in the shed. 2. My daughter's giggle always makes me laugh. 3. Dave wrote his brother's name on the emergency form. 4. The announcement could hardly be heard over the fans' noise. 5. Sarah adjusted the brakes on her sister's bike. 6. An aide picked up the governor's suitcase. 7. This exam will test the students' basic skills. 8. The two candidates' speeches were similar. 9. Marcus's score was the highest in the class. 10. Work was done on the women's locker room.

Page 196

1. B, 2. F, 3. C, 4. J, 5. A, 6. J, 7. B, 8. G

Writing Friendly Letters
Page 197

1. heading: *April 12, 2005* 2. closing: *With love,* 3. salutation: *Dear Mary Ann,* 4. signature: printed name is not used in friendly letter

Page 198

Heading: *June 22, 2005;* **salutation:** *Dear Sasha,* **body:** *How are you? I'm wondering what your plans are for the rest of the summer. I'd love to have you come for a visit if you can get away for a few days. Let me know what your schedule looks like.* **closing:** *Sincerely yours,* **signature:** *Roger*

Page 199

Answers will vary. Sample answer:
Heading: *November 12, 2005;* **salutation:** *Dear Aunt Becky,* **body:** *I'm taking a quick break from work to write to you. I brought my lunch and am sitting in the plaza across from my office building. It's unseasonably warm, and I'm going to enjoy this sun while we have it.* (new paragraph) *I hope you're having nice weather too. I'm really looking forward to seeing you and Uncle Morris at Thanksgiving. I hope you'll bring your famous creamed onions. I remember when I was little, everybody laughed at me for liking onions better than pumpkin pie. See you soon.* **Closing:** *Yours truly,* **Signature:** *Deborah*

Page 200

1. C, 2. G, 3. B, 4. F, 5. D, 6. H

Writing Business Letters
Page 201

1. Closing; Yours truly, 2. Heading; June 3, 2004, 3. Inside Address, P.O. Box 145

Page 202

Heading: May 29, 2005
Inside address: Wacky Websites Company 1719 Enterprise Parkway, Houston, TX 77573 **Salutation:** Dear Human Resources Director: **Body:** I recently earned a certificate in Web design and am seeking a job in the computer field. In addition to knowing how to make Web sites, I am familiar with many software programs. Please consider me for the job advertised in the newspaper last Sunday. **Closing:** Yours truly, **Signature:** *Everett Thomas,* **Name:** Everett Thomas

Page 203

Heading, date, wording of body of letter, and closing will vary but must be capitalized and punctuated correctly.
Inside address: (*line 1*) Traver Photography (*line 2*) 3621 Bedford Street (*line 3*) Tomahawk, WI 54487 **Greeting:** Dear Ms. Traver:

Page 204

1. C, **2.** J, **3.** B, **4.** G, **5.** A, **6.** F

Assessment

Pages 206–208

1. A, **2.** G, **3.** B, **4.** H, **5.** D, **6.** J, **7.** C, **8.** F, **9.** A, **10.** G, **11.** D, **12.** G, **13.** C, **14.** H, **15.** D, **16.** H, **17.** B, **18.** H, **19.** C, **20.** F